three generations west

SAGA of the SOO

VOLUME II

An illustrated history of the Soo Line Railroad and its
predecessors in Minnesota, the Dakotas and Montana.

By **JOHN A. GJEVRE**

**With Contributing Authors
Patrick Dorin, Carol Monroe,
William Sherman, John Tunheim**

THE RECLUSIVE PRAIRIE

A seldom seen Soo Line 2-6-2 "Prairie" class locomotive traverses the late afternoon frozen countryside
with a mixed consist. Built in 1907, engine #802 was one of only ten on the Soo Line roster.

Front piece painting by Larry Fisher

ISBN   0-9646134-0-9

The type for this book was set in Truetype™ Times, Middleton and Helvetica by Peter Gjevre who also produced the book design with additional assistance by Sandra Kay Designs who did the paging. Color separations and black and white half tone negatives were made by Dakota Photographics. Camera–ready laser output was produced by Whiskey Creek Document Design. Cover art by Larry Fisher. Printed in Fargo, ND by Knight Printing.

Published by: Agassiz Publications
P.O.Box 112
Moorhead, MN 56561-0112

Also by the same author:
Saga of the Soo, Part I: West From Shoreham 1973, 1990

Chili Line, the narrow rail trail to Santa Fe 1969, 1971
An illustrated history of the Denver, Rio Grande Western narrow gauge branch line
from Antonito to Santa Fe, 1880-1941

Dedicated to Karen and Stuart

and to the memory of Wayne Olsen

Soo Line Railroad

Don Mahoney

From 1883 the Soo (phonetic for Sault) has been a dependable, adaptable and distinctive railroad. Never quite romantic, it faced rather few obstacles (other than weather, finances and the lack of traffic). It was to have its birth in Minneapolis as the Minneapolis, Sault Ste. Marie and Atlantic Ry. With its westward-bound sister, the Minneapolis and Pacific Ry. and others, it merged with the financial help of the Canadian Pacific in 1888 to become the M.St.P. & S.S.M.Ry. as per the stock certificate above. Suffering bankruptcy in 1937, it reemerged as the M.St.P. & S.M.RR. of 1944 thereafter merging with the Wisconsin Central and the Duluth, South Shore and Atlantic in 1961. After purchasing the Minneapolis, Northfield & Southern and the Milwaukee Road, its traffic and character gradually evolved. It was to change again in 1990 when it was purchased outright by its parent company Canadian Pacific. The passenger ad to the right is symbolic of the imagination of a traffic department for a line that solely served very few population centers. 67653 (an Ortner Car covered gondola delivered in 1962) represents the adaptability of a granger road that increasingly serves America's industrial heartland as well as the prairies and steppes of North Dakota.

Here is sport for Spartans,
Speeding o'er the plain,
Dashing into sunshine,
Thro' a wall of rain.
Racing with the tempest,
Yes! and winning too!
Nothing earthly, equals
Riding on the Soo.

SOO LINE

2 STEEL TRAINS 2 Between St. Paul Minneapolis and Duluth Superior DAILY (Electric Lighted and Vacuum Cleaned)

Soo Line Railroad

TABLE of CONTENTS

Foreword

John Gjevre has assembled interesting details of local community histories and has neatly woven them into an excellent pictorial history of the Soo. *Three Generations West* appropriately describes the focal point of the book --- three generations of pictures from the 1890s to the present.

Those who are nostalgic about the small country towns that once dotted rural America every eight miles will thoroughly enjoy the views of main street. The ever present grain elevators - sentinals of the wheat country, with the depot nearby, churches, schools, hotels, general merchandise stores, blacksmith shops, and banks are still vivid in the minds of many people who grew up in those communities. At the end of the twentieth century only a small percentage of our population still has those memories. The others must enjoy them from this excellent collection of well documented photographs.

Three Generations West covers three distinct regions of the Dakotas and Minnesota. The iron ore lines, which were in use from 1911 to 1984, portray an era of greatness for northeastern Minnesota.

The lines that ran through north central Minnesota and to Winnipeg extended through the forest region. Timber loading sidings, instead of steam shovels, were the focal point of these towns.

The third region served by the Soo in the three-state area included the grain and cattle country. Grain elevators, stockyards and the lineside water towers for the Soo's iron horses dominated those communities.

A brief history of each community, interspersed with stories of those who made their careers working for the Soo Line gives the reader of *Three Generations West* the experience of a travelogue of days gone by.

The advertisements, accounts of changing technology, and pictures that encompass a century remind us that conditions are not static. Hundreds of tiny isolated communities have already faded into the past. John Gjevre has caught a glimpse of those bygone villages and some that are still in the process of fading away. Each passing year will add to the value of this excellent collection of pictures and lively accounts of those who lived and worked in these villages and the Soo, which served as the sinew to hold them together.

Hiram M. Drache, Ph.D.
Historian-in-Residence
Concordia College

National Geographic — July 1912

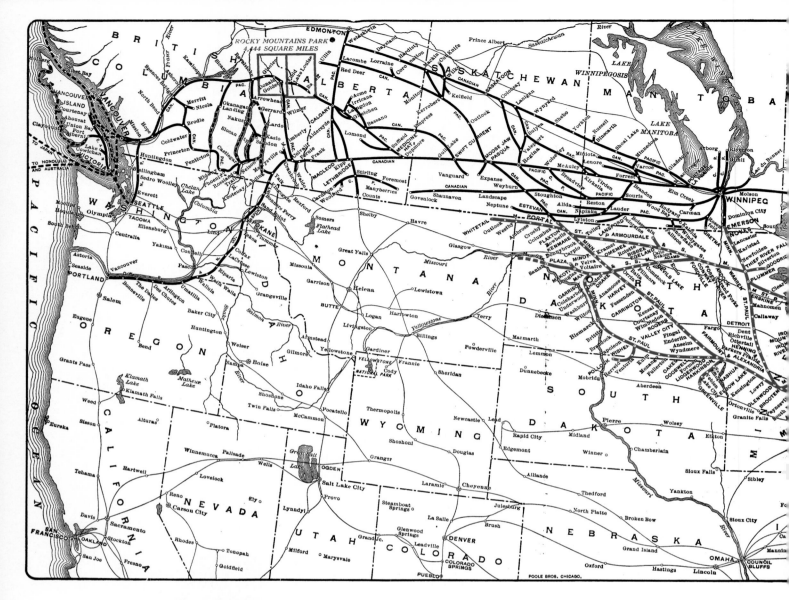

Preface

Many railroad books provide a large amount of information and pictures about transport itself–the motive power, railroad people and personalities, the roadbed and signaling, structures and rolling stock. It has been my hope that this current volume will provide an informative text along with maps, photographs, artwork, tables and examples of advertisements about the historic Soo throughout three generations. Specific additional information about the line's economic base, its relationship to its parent road the Canadian Pacific as well as the Minneapolis, Northfield and Southern Railway and the Milwaukee Road was outlined in *Volume I* and will be expanded in forthcoming *Volume III* in this series.

It is my wish that material about geography, geology and societal factors impacting on line placement and operations for the Soo Line in Minnesota, the Dakotas and northwestern Montana will be of interest to the public as well as those special folk who

claim the Soo as 'their' railroad. The initial chapter deals with the overall geography of the area served by the Soo north and west of Minneapolis/St. Paul. Some knowledge of the terrain as well as the area's productivity and population should help clarify reasons for certain Soo Line strengths and weaknesses.

In addition, this book places pictorial emphasis on the differences in operations, personnel responsibilities and equipment throughout the three generations in which the Soo has served the Upper Midwest.

Strictly speaking there is no longer an entity called the Soo in 1995. The beginning of the end of the Soo Line age occurred some 107 years ago. It was then the Canadian Pacific and its financiers came to the rescue of the young and struggling carrier which led to the 1888 consolidation.

The not necessarily sad death of the Soo dates to the complete ownership (through stock purchase) of the Soo Line Corporation by the CP in 1990.

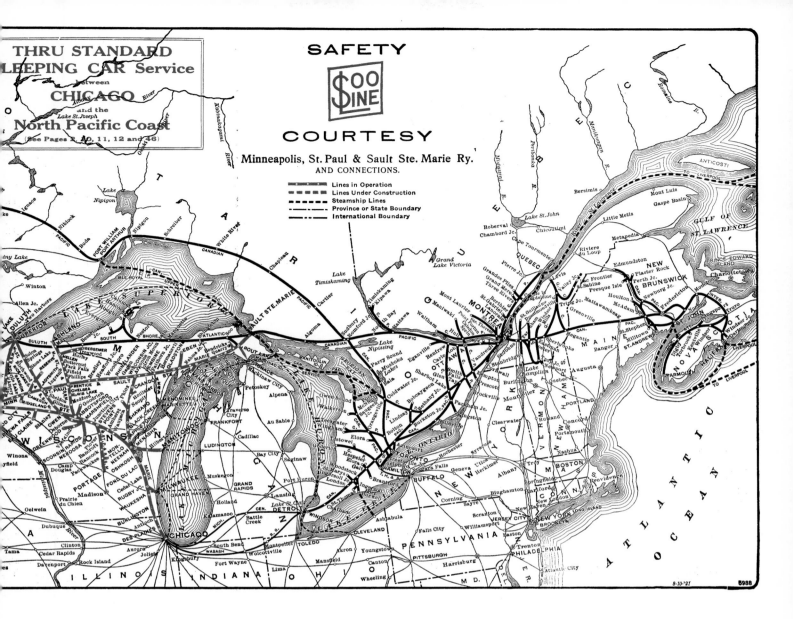

Today, the road, rails and facilities remain much the same as before, however; paychecks, business cards, letterheads and locomotives are now labeled Canadian Pacific.

Locomotives labeled SOO traverse Canada and the old Delaware and Hudson line. Similarly, Canadian Pacific units appear with ever increasing frequency throughout Soo Line Land. At this time all new motive power and equipment as well as newly repainted locomotives are labeled with the CP logo.

Finally, the reader will find information in *Volume II* as well as a forthcoming *Volume III* about specific operations or industries which either provided lading or support to the Soo. Examples in this volume include the North American Creameries, the Barrett ice harvest, the Cuyuna Iron Range and ore docks at Superior, along with coal docks and coaling towers, stock traffic and stockyards and the maintenance support throughout the line. We are grateful for Patrick Dorin's willingness to share his special expertise about the iron ore traffic.

Yet - there is much more history to preserve. It seems imperative that additional information should be developed and presented in what I hope will be the third volume in this series. You the reader can help finish this needed work with your willingness to share information and material. The Soo is part of our living history right in the very heart of the Upper Midwest. Please write me if you can help, or share your treasured information with the Soo Line Historical and Technical Society. This organization has over a thousand men and women finding, sharing, and preserving information about the Soo and its related roads.

Errors and omissions are solely my responsibility. Even though I have avoided using previously published photos, there are several pictures which either appeared in the 1st edition of *Saga of the Soo Volume I* (published in 1973), or Patrick Dorin's *The Soo Line* or in Judge Suprey's *Steam Trains of the Soo*. These 'reused' photos have added specific information or serve as examples of equipment or service when I was unaware of an unpublished alternative. In addition, an advertisement or two have been reused.

References in the text are keyed to *Part I* (Second edition) and the index at the end of this volume addresses both *Part I* (2nd ed.) as well as *Part II*. Hopefully the reader will have access to *Saga of the Soo Part I: West from Shoreham* (2nd ed. 1990) as this volume is read.

Finally, in order to reduce confusion and have a uniformity of style, I have taken the convention of using the terms Soo, Soo Line or Soo Line Railroad to interchangeably mean the old Soo (Minneapolis, St. Paul and Sault Ste. Marie Ry. or RR), the Soo Line Railroad, the CP/Soo and the CP-US Heavy Haul. Where CP or Canadian Pacific is used it means the parent road in Canada regardless of the year or time period.

John A. Gjevre
Moorhead, Minnesota
March 1994

Below: Soo crews are cutting through a sandstone hill in downtown Minneapolis during 1892. The old union depot with its spire is seen in the distance.

Extending the Soo Line

E. Gross photo, Paul Carlson Collection

Above: Soo rail machine at work on the Wheat Line near Kenmare in 1905. Typically, outside contractors would do the grading and bridge work as new lines were laid out, but the railroad used its own crews for placing ties, rail and ballast.

Minnesota Historical Society

Prologue

The purposes of this chapter are to relate how geography, geology and climate influenced the Soo's decision to construct its lines and methods of operation. Although there had been settlement prior to the railroad's presence, it can be understood that advertising did influence settlement choices. The fact that railroads advertised widely has always been appreciated; yet we realize that individual land and real estate firms did benefit themselves as well as the Soo with their advertising efforts. It should be said that these activities were not necessarily sanctioned nor openly supported by the railroad.

Colonel Clement A. Lounsberry moved to Fargo, North Dakota during the 1880's and was to make a profitable business of boosting North Dakota immigration and settlement. He wrote articles and published *the Record* which detailed stories of successful men and groups of settlers throughout North Dakota. Language used by Lounsberry was always eloquent, flowery, positive and enthusiatic. This author wonders how many settler's children rued the day their parents were lured to the steppes of the Dakota plains after the harsh realities of the thirties hit the state. For many, the struggle to remain on the prairie was beyond their mettle.

Geography, more so than geology, influences a railroad's route, grade, equipment and style. Geology in the form of mineral wealth (including soil type and suitability) will, however, influence traffic and the economic growth or decline of a line.

Since the *Saga of the Soo* series hopes to chronicle the times of the Soo Line to the north and west of the Twin Cities - we will confine these pages to the geographic history and geology of Minnesota and the Dakotas.

One's understanding of the geography of Soo Line land might best start with knowledge regarding the actions of the Laurentide ice sheet which covered almost all of Canada, most of Minnesota, North Dakota and northeastern Montana during the last ice age. We are told that this huge glacier occurred 9,000 to 16,000 years ago. The glacier carved, scarred and leveled the land while transporting debris both from the actual pressure of the ice as well as from melt water as the climate warmed and the ice receded north.

As the ice retreated some 13,000 years ago, the glacier in central and northern Manitoba became a dam which prevented waters from flowing north (to what is known today as Hudson's Bay). Thus was formed an enormous lake - glacial Lake Agassiz. This lake initially drained to the south and east through the ancient glacial River Warren, which carved out today's Minnesota River Valley.

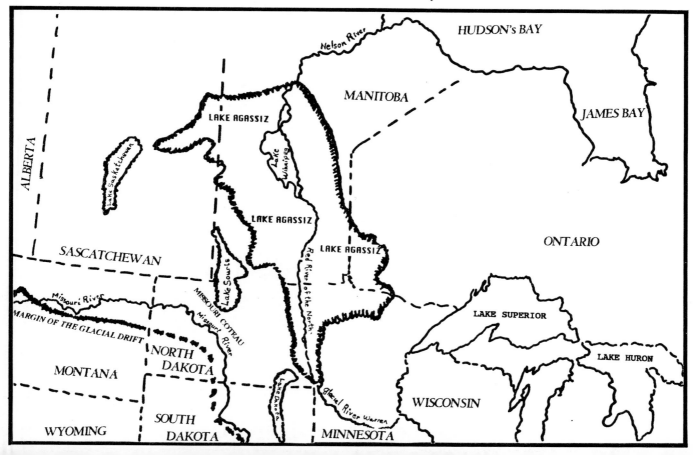

Over perhaps 3000 years the mean temperature slowly rose, causing the glacier(s) to melt. The lake level rose and fell in response to a highly complex interaction of events including global warming at that time. Thus were formed a series of beaches which today have abundant sedimentary sand and gravel. The striking flatness of our Red River Valley today and its remarkable fertility is a reminder of that long ago lake bottom. The beaches are named for towns or areas where a rise with sand and gravel was early discovered such as Herman, Tintah, Campbell and others. These beaches can have both postive and negative economic values: i.e. sand and gravel deposits in many areas versus the sand dune areas which cannot sustain reasonable tillage agriculture. The Sheyenne National Grasslands are but one example of the negative economic impact of the retreating glacier.

Even today, the action of ice jams during spring runoff cause flooding in the Red River Valley. This is quite easily understood since the Red flows north and spring thaws start south in March and work northward. Results of Red River fury (caused by a slow melt in Manitoba) against the Soo can be observed on page 51, *Part I.*

During the time the Laurentide ice sheet was retreating to the northeast over present day Lake Superior, the waters so trapped formed glacial Lake Duluth. This partly drained through the Moose River near Moose Lake. This in turn drained into what is the present day St. Croix River (which today forms the northern boundary between Minnesota and Wisconsin).

During this same time frame, to the west in North Dakota were two additional glacial lakes whose lake bottoms today provide fertile prairies for farming. These were Lake Souris, north and east of Minot as well as ancient Lake Dakota beginning in southeastern North Dakota and extending into South Dakota.

The moraines and hills so prominent along the western main line of the Soo are noted in those sections in this volume. Glacial drift has both covered and uncovered vast deposits of lignite coal in central and western North Dakota. Today this coal is mined for power generation nearby the minehead. Present day coal reserves are mind boggling. Hopefully, technological advances will allow preprocessing of the lignite so it can be economically transported long distances by the Soo (Canadian Pacific) to energy gobbling population centers throughout the United States and Canada. Indeed, long term prospects for energy enrichment would allow a lignite product to be transported to the Twin Ports for shipment via the Great Lakes to European markets; there are many who fear that the abandonment of the Brooten line to Superior may have long term negative economic impact upon the Soo.

Quite obviously there are no true mountains in Soo Line Land, and for the most part the grades are fairly gentle and braking was never a serious problem. For that reason few Soo diesels are equipped with dynamic braking. With the acquisition of the Milwaukee Road in 1985, however, the Soo inherited a number of high horsepower units with dynamic brakes.

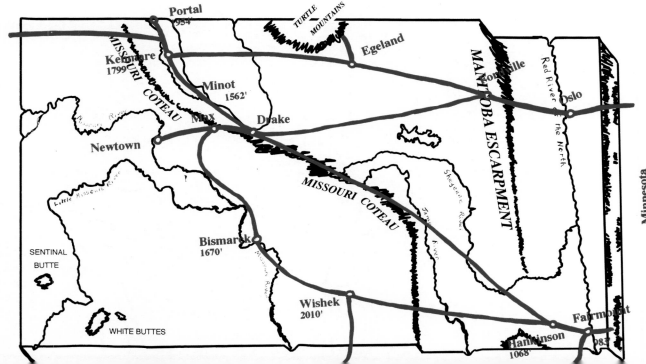

W.R. Callaway was general passenger agent for the Soo about the turn of the century. He was able to get press releases into the Northwest Newspaper Union which supplied 'boilerplate articles' for numerous publications at that time. Such was printed by news hungry publishers without any specific hint it was advertising. Listen to his modest (?) boasting from 1898 in *The Record*: "...*The prairies of North Dakota are covered with a rich, dark drift of alluvial loam from one to four feet deep, under which is a clay subsoil which has the property of holding moisture to a wonderful degree and giving it out as needed for the growing crops. It contains practically inexhaustible supplies of the soil ingredients most valuable for agriculture, namely soluble silica, lime, potash, soda, phosphoric acid, nitrogen and vegetable humus. There is no better soil in the world for general farming purposes — and after the prairie sod is once broken, cultivation is done with comparatively little labor....The stock industry is in its infancy, but there is no country where stock is more healthy or thrives better — especially along the Mouse and Des Lacs Rivers in Ward County.*"

Callaway goes on in the same release (printed in numerous weekly and monthly newspapers) about the favorable conditions for dairying with good grazing, abundant water and convenient markets. Also found in this same release *"A large part of the surface of western North Dakota is underlaid with veins of lignite coal....The Soo Railway traverses for seventy miles the valleys (of these coal seams) and distributes this cheap fuel at low rates."*

His comments about Dakota climate, however exaggerated, bear much truth even one hundred years later. *"The objection is frequently made by the home seeker that the climate of the Northwest is too cold to live in and be successful. It is not strange that residents of the [East] --- should be chilled to the bone in the damp atmosphere of those regions at a temperature of five to twelve below zero Fahrenheit should think they would perish at minus thirty. People [who are] dressed to ride in the cold of the Middle and New England states and [are] shivering with cold at ten, or even five below zero will, if dressed the same will be comfortable in North Dakota at 30 degrees below on a calm still day. ---It is the lightness, dryness and purity of the atmosphere that makes the climate of Minnesota and North Dakota one the most delightful and healthy to live in. Fever and ague and other zymotic diseases are practically unknown. Physicians are perhaps the only class who complain of their lack of opportunities for business."*

He ends the article (still not appearing to be an ad since it was not a paid insertion) by noting that the Soo Railway, *"has no land grant but aids in the development of the country by granting half rates to bona fide land seekers."* Advertisements made by the Soo in those days tended to follow the style or format of those displayed on these pages. However; on page 141 *Part I*, it can be seen that the Soo continued to promote land settlement as late as 1922.

Farmers were not to be the only settlers the Soo encouraged and aided with migration and colonization. Merchants also benefitted by the railway's enticements. Elevator companies received special concessions early-on with lease arrangements for railroad owned land along sidings. In all newly developing villages the Soo or its land agent was more that happy to provide lumberyards with a free site and sometimes reduced inbound rates in order to stimulate building, both in the villages as well as on farms.

A Modern Railway

3/10 of one per cent Grade.
3000 Ties to the Mile.
80-pound Steel Rails.
16-foot Road Bed.
Gravel Ballast.
Modern Passenger Equipment.
Dining Car Service.
Buffet Library Service.
Comfortable Sleeping Cars.

Scenic Through Car Routes

TWIN CITIES—WINNIPEG.
TWIN CITIES—BOSTON.
TWIN CITIES—NORTH PACIFIC.

TWIN CITIES TO WINNIPEG, FIFTEEN HOURS.

TWIN CITIES TO WINNIPEG, FIFTEEN DAYS.

A Modern Railway
3/10 of one per cent Grade.

As noted in *Part I* pp 136-137, the Soo Line, along with its competitors, the GN and NP, had their educational trains as well as experimental and test farms. These railroad agricultural agents encouraged improved livestock and grain production methods long before the county agents were here. These "extension" services existed strictly at railroad expense and almost never made a direct profit to the line. Furthermore, as noted in the stockyard section in this volume, cattlemen were allowed free passage with stock movements. This 'goodwill' measure proved a real money maker for the Soo inasmuch as it did not need to use its own employees to take cattle and sheep off the trains for mandatory rest and watering.

Without a doubt the Soo truly considered colonization to have many stages. After the initial influx, it was mandatory that the settler become a permanent resident of Minnesota or the Dakotas. Only contented townsfolk and farmers would strive to build an economic base to provide the young railroad with ongoing growth. The example of the Soo building immigration buildings in Kenmare for landseekers and new settlers to live temporarily is but one good will effort mentioned in a later chapter. That the railway and its land development agent often donated land for churches and schools undoubtably helped to encourage the settlement and provide it with a sense of community. The distribution of blooded stock to ranchers and dairymen has been noted in *Part I*. It was not only the Soo, but also Jim Hill's Great Northern that encouraged the development of good roads - the very death angel to rail passenger service.

1946

1914

MINNEAPOLIS.

Minneapolis is known the world over as the "Flour City" and its flour goes to every corner of the globe. The unparalleled water power of St. Anthony's Falls together with the city's geographical position have developed this industry from a clumsy mill with a few barrels capacity to a daily output of 80,000 barrels, the greatest of any city in the world.

While the manufacture of flour has established the city's reputation abroad its lumber production also is the greatest of any city in the world. The maximum output of lumber was in 1899 when it exceeded 594,000,000 feet and in 1903 was 432,000,000 feet. Around this wonderful nucleus has been gathered a great manufacturing and jobbing center which embraces all lines of trade, especially those contingent on the grain and flour market and the grain producing territory tributary.

Nearly every agricultural machinery house in the country has a distributing branch in Minneapolis and many have their own substantial buildings. The city itself produced over $6,000,000 worth of agricultural machinery, etc., in 1901.

Minneapolis is the natural market for the products of Minnesota, North Wisconsin, North Dakota and South Dakota and consequently the great distributing center from which these products reach the balance of the country and the foreign market. Transportation facilities are pressed to the limit and much of the traffic moves through the Great Lakes via Duluth and other ports. The "SOO LINE" is the only Minneapolis road with its own line of steamers on the Great Lakes and with its all rail and lake and rail connections affords the short route to the seaboard.

THE NEW "SOO LINE" GENERAL OFFICE BUILDING
MINNEAPOLIS

PIKE & COOK.
BUILDERS

H. KELLY & CO.
HEATING, PLUMBING AND VENTILATION

MENOMONIE HYDRAULIC PRESSED BRICK CO.
BRICK

Soo Line Railroad

Red, white and black–a pair of SD 40-2's forge west from Minneapolis to Glenwood and north only to battle more Minnesota snow. Winter 1985

Some breakdowns require 'on the road' repairs. Certainly a burned out headlight mandates attention. July, 1991: Mainline North Dakota

J. David Ingles

The Large Ones of the Line

4008, a dual purpose Mountain locomotive built by the American Locomotive works for the Wisconsin Central and used all over the Soo Line. This was one of 21 similar engines having 69" drivers (three of which were built in the Soo's own Shoreham shops). These engines saw service pulling heavy freights on the mainline as well as summer assignments on the Mountaineer.

Soo Line Railroad

6062, the last new power purchased by the Soo (in 1989) prior to the Canadian Pacific takeover during January of 1990. Five SD 60's were equipped with the 'comfort cab' as pictured. All were delivered in the attractive candy-apple red scheme. December 1989

Soo Line Railroad

Soo Wheels Help Keep Mill Wheels Turning in
"Master Miller" MINNEAPOLIS

No halfway measures for Minneapolis; the burning energy that typifies its every undertaking has marvelous stamina—has made Minneapolis the metropolis of the Upper Midwest.

ANOTHER THRIVING CITY IN Soo Line Land

Dramatically emphasizing the 22 lakes, 151 parks in Minneapolis is this skyline view. The city has built a strong industrial core while holding fast to its natural beauty. Industry—ably served by the Soo—has grown mightily, turning out a host of products that span the earth. Yet Minneapolis still has room to grow—still has room for new business. For information on industrial sites contact Mr. R. S. Claar, Soo Line, Minneapolis 2.

From the beginning of Minneapolis, flour milling has been an important industry. One of the first buildings constructed in the new town was a mill. Three factors made flour a natural for Minneapolis—nearby wheat fields, abundant water power and rail links to eastern markets. Today Minneapolis produces more than 13 *billion* pounds of flour each year, plus countless other cereal and bakery products—and is headquarters for the world's five leading flour companies. The Soo Line, one of Minneapolis' major railroads, hauls to and from these giant mills and most of the other industries in humming Minneapolis.

Humming factories—more than 1300 of them—dot Minneapolis, the 13th ranking industrial center in America. Farm machinery and implements, hearing aids and pumps, iron and steel products, electronic controls and linseed derivatives, paints and varnishes, thermostats and lingerie, electric motors and machinery, generators and outboard motors, clothing and appliances, escalator parts and hydraulic lifts—all these and many more come from Minneapolis.

Nicollet Avenue is the retail heart of Minneapolis and center of trade for two million people. Retail trade tops $800 million a year putting Minneapolis second in per capita retail sales in America, tenth in total retail sales. Wholesale volume exceeds $2.5 billion annually. Minneapolis is the nation's summer sports center during the ten-day Aquatennial Carnival when more than two million persons crowd into Minneapolis for the fun, many of them traveling by Soo Line.

Ship *SOO* if you ship to or thru
THE UPPER MIDWEST

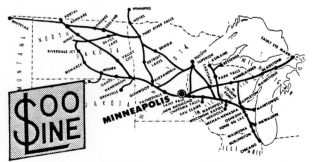

—your working partner 7 days a week

Minneapolis

The early history of the Soo Line is best understood by the grain milling industry which started about 1859 along St. Anthony Falls (on the Mississippi in today's downtown Minneapolis). The Cataract mill was built about this time on the west bank of the Missisippi. W.D. Washburn, who was to head the drive to create the Soo and who became its first president, was at that time secretary of the Minneapolis Mill Company (for further information about W.D. Washburn, see *Saga of the Soo Part I* pp 203-204). He founded Washburn Mill Company, which successively became Washburn Crosby Company, and eventually the General Mills of today.

THE PILLSBURY COMPANY

After George B. Christian and Company introduced the middlings' purifier to flour milling, it became possible to produce a superior flour from hard spring wheat—the type that grows well in the Red River Valley, North Dakota, Montana, and Canada. In 1878, the first experimental mill was fitted with rollers for grinding flour. This allowed production capacity to increase dramatically and the transition from millstones to roller mills occurred rapidly.

Charles A. Pillsbury arrived in Minneapolis in 1869, and starting in 1870 he owned a single mill having a capacity of 300 barrels per day. Today, the Pillsbury Company (no longer owned by the Pillsburys) is an international business giant.

During the 1870's, efforts were made to stimulate the export trade and some years later Minneapolis mills were exporting 5,000,000 barrels a year.

In early days, flour was always packed and shipped in barrels, each weighing 196 pounds. In 1900, about half of the flour was still shipped in barrels. By 1920, however, the barrel disappeared in favor of cotton

bags of standard sizes. Today it is possible to purchase flour in such small amounts as two pounds, however most grocery store consumers usually buy their flour in ten or twenty-five pound bags (bags today are, of course, of paper).

A great deal of flour goes directly to commercial bakeries, as well as to the production of prepared and prefabricated foods. Much of this flour is shipped via rail in airslide hopper cars.

Although Pillsbury and General Mills still have their headquarters in the Minneapolis area, much production of flour has shifted to the east. Minneapolis is no longer known as the *Flour City*.

Below: **353**–an RS-1, 1000 hp Alco road switcher–slightly in need of a wash job at Shoreham in the original maroon and gold.

Lloyd Berger Jr.

Soo Line Railroad

Diesel shops at Shoreham around 1967. Note the spacious work area; two GP 3's are on the left and **415**, one of the Alco Dolly sisters, sits at left.

Note that the Chevrolet road/railer was already equipped with 'ditchlights' more than 25 years before Soo Locomotives began to be so equipped for running north of the international boundary.

Soo Line Railroad

301, *one of the very earliest* diesel units on the Soo system. This is a 1000 hp EMD-NW-2 purchased in 1939. It balances on the Shoreham turntable on May 29, 1962.

Lloyd Berger Jr.

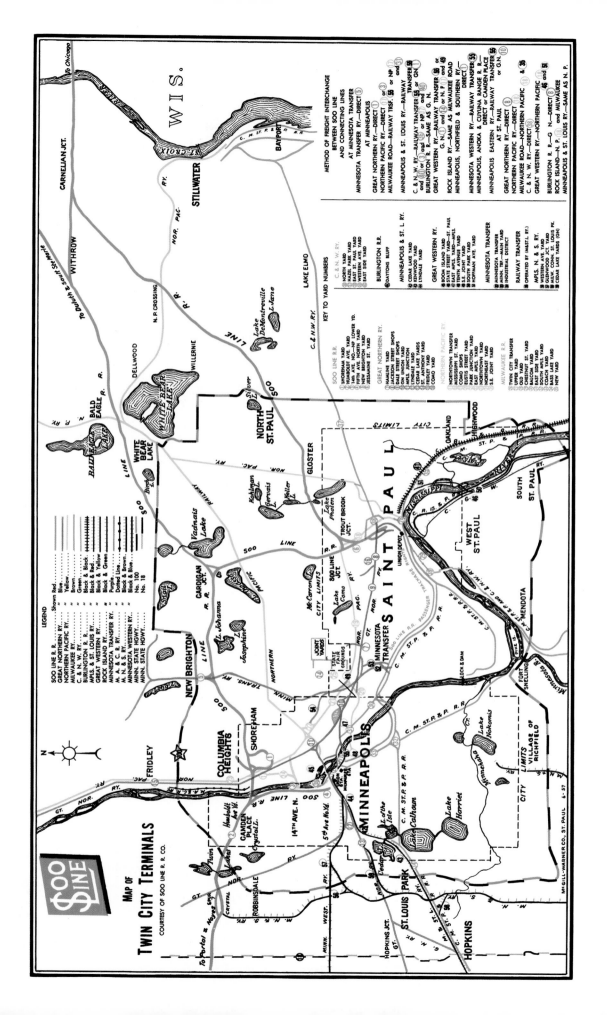

MAP OF
TWIN CITY TERMINALS
COURTESY OF SOO LINE R. R. CO.

Above: view of Shoreham yards from the east taken over 2nd Avenue NE showing Central Avenue running left to right past the Roundhouse (see page 156, *Part I* for details, and also page 7, *Part I* for another aerial photo of the area).

Soo Line Railroad

Below: Shoreham 1926, the tree and low shop building in the center were long gone by the time the above photo was taken.

Minnesota Historical Society

Shoreham

The Shoreham yards and shops in northeast Minneapolis served as the main terminal for the Soo for about 100 years. The Wisconsin Central (leased by the Soo in 1909) had yards on Boom Island on the Mississippi River near downtown Minneapolis. These were sold and Wisconsin Central operations were amalgamated into the Soo as its Chicago Division. Today's Wisconsin Central Ltd. is almost a rebirth of the old Wisconsin Central after it had purchased most Soo Line trackage in Wisconsin and Northern Michigan.

GP30 entering Shoreham from the East circa 1964.
Soo Line Railroad

Excellent pictorial coverage of the Shoreham Shops can be found in *Saga of the Soo Part I* pp 156-163 These shops were famed for their varied capabilities; here were three Mountain type locomotives (4018, 4019 and 4020 each weighing 345,000 lbs,) erected during the dark times of the nation's depression. These shops had many diverse abilities such that not only were passenger cars serviced and overhauled at Shoreham in Northeast Minneapolis, but in addition complete rebuilds and modernization of nearly complete passenger trains were accomplished. The Soo Line passenger trains were never lightweight and streamlined, nonetheless they were efficiently up to date and reliable. (The last new trainset of passenger cars was for the 1928 Winnipegger.) The Shoreham rebuilds helped keep the Soo competitive on the Chicago-Duluth service and the Minneapolis-Winnipeg runs in the years following World War II. The name 'Shoreham' comes from W.D. Washburn's favorite summering place in Maine.

Through the years many changes have come to Shoreham - the large classification yards 'A' and 'B' have closed and have been torn up, in favor of using the much more modern 'Pigs Eye' yard of the former Milwaukee Road along the Mississippi in Saint Paul. The former passenger shops and yard are but a memory. Intermodal yards for truck and container traffic have now found their home at Shoreham and an auto transport yard is in nearby Arden Hills. Following the CP purchase in 1990, very heavy locomotive repair and painting are done north of the border.

The wheel shop at Shoreham has for over a century repaired and rehabilitated wheel sets. All cars today use roller bearings and have steel wheels. The roller bearings are disassembled and cleaned here whilst the wheels themselves are checked with magnetic and ultrasound testing before being remounted on the axles and refinished. Between five and ten special flat cars for transport of wheelsets will carry these rehabilitated sets to the far corners of Soo Line land.

A small vignette about the power house at Shoreham will help the reader understand the self sufficiency of the main shops of the Soo. Starting around 1890, steam boilers were erected to provide heating for the entire complex via a network of underground steam lines. These same boilers were to power several steam engines that provided lighting and equipment power (220 volt DC) plus a 100 kw AC alternator for emergency power in addition to a huge shop air compressor. The largest installation was made in 1905 when three Buckeye-Westinghouse engine generator sets were installed with DC capacities of 100, 200, and 300 kilowatts each. The smallest steam engine (100 kw) was belted to a standby AC generator for emergency power when the commercial power (Northern States Power) was down. These three engines were of cross compound type - noncondensing, but the exhaust steam was used to heat an open feedwater heater. An 1895 Ingersoll-Sargeant and an 1905 Ingersoll-Rand steam engine/ aircompressor (cross compound/Corliss type) easily provided the entire complex with steam at 100 p.s.i.

June 30, 1967 and September 4, 1941 saw the Shoreham area in northeaast Minneapolis visited by most unwelcome windstorms and tornados which heavily damaged buildings, yards and cars. The 1941 destruction is depicted in photos on page 163 *Saga of the Soo Part I.*

Watercolor by John Cartwright

A westbound time freight at the Crystal tower–approximately seven miles northwest of Shoreham. Here Soo tracks cross the original main line of the Great Northern to St. Cloud, Alexandria and west. During the 1940s and 50s at least six Soo passenger trains plus sometimes ten or more GN passenger trains and an equal number of freight trains passed this point daily. In the distance is the U.S. 52 highway overpass.

Along the Missisippi in downtown Minneapolis a trio of geeps pass the impressive Minneapolis post office.

Soo Line Railroad

As the Twin Cities grew, industrial expansion was fostered by the Soo. American Hoist and Derrick in St.Paul, for example, was served by the Soo as well as by the Minneapolis milling district. After World War II industrial parks were established in response to the twin needs of urban planning along with railroad's wishes of having short and accessible industrial trackage.

The purchase of the Minneapolis, Northfield and Southern Railway in 1982 added some 130 industries alone to the Soo. Purchase of the Chicago Great Western Railway by the Chicago North-Western Railway resulted in trackage rights for the Soo over former CGW tracks to the Roseport industrial area South of Saint Paul. Additional industrial expansion in the sixties and early seventies brought new plants to Soo centers in Arden Hills and New Brighton. In 1969, for instance, International Paper alone added a 157,000 square foot plant in Arden Hills.

Minneapolis Steel Machinery Company along Minneapolis Lake Street was one of many industries that served midwestern and Canadian farmers. It later became Minneapolis Moline. The plant has closed and very little farm machinery is made in the Twin Cities today. The above load of threshing machines and tractors on a Canadian Pacific flat car is bound for Western Canada via the Soo in 1920.

Minnesota Historical Society

Below: Soo line shop forces receive on the job training at Shoreham about 1910. Instruction, development and training has always been necessary, and with today's quickly moving technology, is mandatory for any railroad in order to remain competitive.

Soo Line Railroad

Shoreham Vignettes

Below: The September 1941 Tornado hit Northeast Minneapolis and Shoreham hard, very hard.

Soo Line Railroad

1218 switches CP business car on the Shoreham turntable.

Soo Line Railroad

Baldwin 397 DT 6-6-2000 a 2000 hp heavy switch engine from the Duluth, South Shore and Atlantic at Shoreham 10-18-66. Only these Baldwins had the Soo Line spelled out completely in the 'new' locomotive livery.

Dennis Schmidt

"If only I could run a Pacific. Please, Please...a time machine for my birthday." –at Shoreham 1936.

Minnesota Historical Society

Right: steam on the Soo has been dealt its death blow by Mr. 'Dirty' Diesel. **735**, an H3 Pacific destined for display at Minot has been 'gussied' up by Shoreham shop forces. 6-20-56 at Shoreham.

R. Vierkanz photo, Pete Bonesteel Collection

214, 213, 206, and 558—a single passenger GP-9 points out (facing east) of stall 26 with her Alco and GM freight sisters.

363 Baldwin diesel in the shop for electrical overhaul and airduct modifications in 1955. By this time Shoreham had a dedicated diesel shop.

No! The Soo did not have Beyer-Garrretts, nor did any other U.S. road for that matter, but with the dismantling of steam power in 1955-1956 all sorts of strange things occurred including this pair of L-2 Mikados which were outshopped by Dunkirk in 1920.

Pete Bonesteel Collection

April 21, 1955…and when one thought that only toy trains disconnected their tenders…**431** an F-8 2-8-0 built by Schenectady in 1902 awaits the cutting torch. Its tender will be recycled just as the Soo recycled the ex-Milwaukee GP40 below into fuel tender **4000** some 32 years later.

Pete Bonesteel Collection

Sadly, all the F7's save two are now history, but FP7A **2500** is now at Lake Superior Transportation Museum (Duluth) and has been magnificently restored to the original maroon and gold! Likewise, F7A **2201A** is on display in Ladysmith, Wisconsin.

Soo Line Railroad

To the right is the first fuel tender constructed by Shoreham shops in 1989 from an ex-Milwaukee road GP 40 (outshopped La Grange 1966). The fuel tenders carry 19,000 extra gallons of diesel fuel! and are normally spliced between two S040-2's or SD 60's.

Soo Line Railroad

Symbolically, the new F3 GM diesel from La Grange is nosing in and displacing the not yet tired iron horse in the Shoreham roundhouse. It is the year 1947 and Soo steam will disappear in just eight years.

Soo Line Railroad

Below: **714** – a light Pacific is caught at Shoreham. (4-26-47)

R-74 *-a 1951 Chevrolet* at Shoreham fitted for rail travel. (8-10-51)

John Malven photo, Stuart Nelson Collection

Robert Vierkanz photo, Pete Bonesteel Collection

First Lima Superpower 4-8-4 to grace the Soo's steel ribbons. New in 1938, they moved the tonnage from Minneapolis to Chicago until 1955.

Lawrence Drabus Collection

Right: **105** is double-headed in order to move extra power west. (circa 1950)

John Malven Photo: Stuart Nelson Collection

Below: the Soo terminal elevator under construction at the Humboldt yard in 1916. Line elevators depended on terminal elevators for storage, forwarding, and flexibility.

Stuart Nelson Collection

GP-7 at the Shoreham yards June 1960. The Milwaukee horizontal ribbed box car to the right could be a messenger of things that would happen in 1985.

Tom Straus photo, L.M. Berger Collection

Below: The first new locomotive purchase by the 'New Soo' (after the merger of the M,SPSSM, the Wisconsin Central, and the D.S.S. & A.) were the two Alco RS-27's **415** and **416**. Orphaned as the Soo ceased buying Alco products, they were to remain near the Twin Cities. Here they jointly go through Shoreham's washer. (1963)

Soo Line Railroad

Saint Paul

For most of its years Saint Paul was served from a small yard in the Jessamine Street area. This yard was developed about 1909 after a double track 1218 foot tunnel was carved through the hill from the tracks along the Mississippi Street yard of the Northern Pacific Railway. Passenger traffic from the east and also the Twin Ports came down from either Cardigan Junction or Trout Brook to connect with the Northern Pacific at Soo Line Junction for access to the St. Paul Union Depot. Passenger service from Minneapolis and the west was routed over the Milwaukee Road tracks over the Mississippi and near the University and Midway areas.

Use of the distinctive St. Paul freight house in the Jessamine yard declined during the 1960s and the cessation of less than carload service in 1970 sealed the doom of the yard. During steam days a two stall engine house, a tank and a coaling tower had provided support services for Jessamine.

The 1970 merger of the Northern Pacific with Jim Hill's Great Northern was to make redundant much yard space for the new Burlington Northern. As part of the premerger negotiations, the Soo was allowed to purchase the Mississippi Street yard of the NP. In April 1973 the Soo sought and was granted ICC authority to lease the Mississippi Street yard. This new yard was renamed the Maryland Street yard. From here the Soo services not only the downtown area and the near north industrial district but also industries from Inver Grove to Roseport south of St. Paul that had been on Chicago Great Western trackage. Actual use of this former Northern Pacific yard began June 17, 1974. Soo trains were not really new to Chicago Great Western trackage, since high priority stock trains had trackage rights over the Northern Pacific

Soo Line Railroad

1914 photo of the then new St. Paul freighthouse in Jessamine yard. In later years, a 30 foot high Soo Line 'dollar' sign was illuminated atop the building. It was razed in January, 1984.

as far as the Roberts Street area in downtown St. Paul where they were picked up by CGW Ry. crews to be hauled to the South Saint Paul stockyards.

With the purchase of the bankrupt Milwaukee Road in 1985, the Soo acquired the well engineered Pig's Eye yard complex along the Mississippi River in Saint Paul. Soo trains now go directly through St. Paul on their way to Chicago. Wisconsin Central, Ltd. has the old main line east through North St. Paul to Stevens Point.

The centralization of container traffic, new car and truck haulage, unit grain and potash trains and even unit ethylene gycol trains have served to emphasize how the role of the Soo, like that of most railroads, has

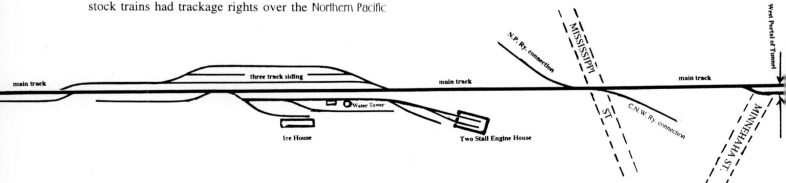

JESSAMINE YARD

shifted from transportation retailer to a wholesaler of transport services. The road participates in lignite coal haul unit trains for electric power generation with the Burlington Northern. The freight houses have closed, the depots are gone and United Parcel Service has supplanted less than carload lading. The forthcoming third volume in this *Saga of the Soo* series will attempt to detail how the Milwaukee Road purchase with its shorter and faster Twin Cities-Chicago route and integration into the Canadian Pacific empire has made the Soo truly part of an International transcontinental route.

SHIPPERS

HELP US KEEP THE CARS ON THE MOVE

7 WAYS TO ASSIST 7

POOL YOUR ORDERS and SHIPMENTS with other concerns in your community.

INCREASE the EFFICIENCY by loading and releasing cars PROMPTLY.

HAVE YOUR SHIPMENT READY for immediate loading on receipt of cars.

BILL YOUR SHIPMENTS THROUGH whenever possible.

RESTRICT your CAR ORDERS to TODAY'S PROGRAM.

DO NOT utilize your FULL FREE TIME.

OBSERVE THE SLOGAN, "LOAD TEN PER CENT ABOVE CAPACITY OF CAR."

RESULTS

Of this cooperation will benefit everybody because it will

SAVE

TIME, LABOR and EQUIPMENT

1911

Pete Bonesteel Collection

Above: The original Union depot in St. Paul was replaced with the present Union depot in 1927. Amtrak passenger trains now stop at the Midway station between the two downtown areas.

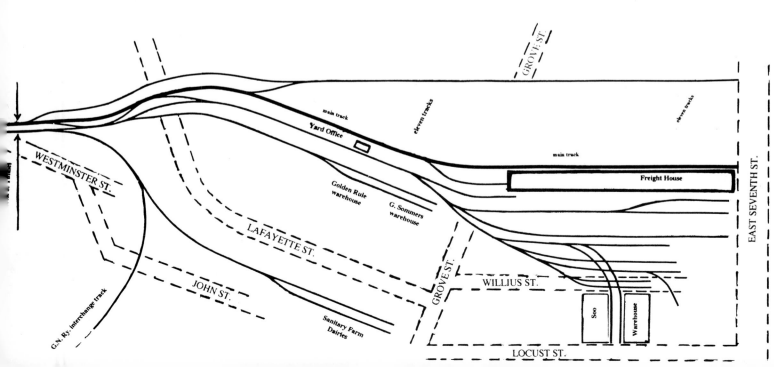

John Malven photo, Stuart Nelson Collection

St. Paul transfer extra 1026 east storms up the hill out of Shoreham past Hi Lo Junction March 15, 1951.

No. 62 at Trout Brook junction in Saint Paul Nov. 18, 1950. Note the special movement of Diner Lounge **2017** which is now on display at the Mid Continent Museum at North Freedom, WI.

John Malven

Commerce, capitol, carnival—and the Soo Line—Prime Movers in

Spirited SAINT PAUL, MINN.

St. Paul goes unpretentiously about its business of being a great commercial city still managing to retain that homespun quality of friendliness which marked its earlier days.

ANOTHER THRIVING CITY IN Soo Line Land

Behind this modern facade lies one of the most varied of American cities. Here is the nation's largest surface abrasive and Cellophane-tape manufacturer; the largest heavy hoist and derrick manufacturer; the country's number one publisher of law-books; the biggest manufacturer of advertising specialties; the largest manufacturer of refrigerators; the biggest producer of air filters for heavy-duty engines; and headquarters for one of the four largest lumber companies in the United States.

Factories blend with landscapes in Saint Paul. This assembly plant for one of the world's largest-selling cars houses the country's only glass-making division within an automobile plant. Also located within the city are one of the five leading publishers of farm periodicals and catalogues; general offices and plant of a large auto and marine storage-battery manufacturer; large breweries whose products are shipped all over America, Canada, South America and Asia; the number one manufacturer of home permanent-wave kits; one of the country's largest branch mail-order houses; and the home offices of one of America's biggest insurance companies.

World-famous livestock markets in South Saint Paul hold first place in dairy cattle and feeder pig receipts; second in all livestock sales. Nearly five million animals are handled here annually; three

million are purchased by local packing plants, and the balance shipped to buyers in 37 states. The Soo Line hauls for many shippers; ranks third in volume of livestock carried to and from this huge market.

Cutting carnival capers are marchers in the Saint Paul winter carnival, the nation's leading winter spectacle. The week-long holiday features winter sports and nationality group festivals.

On a high bluff the Capitol overlooks the entire city to the rolling Mississippi. It has been called one of America's most beautiful capitol buildings. Saint Paul is emphasizing that beauty with a new capitol approach and park system.

More than half a million cars yearly are handled by Minnesota Transfer, one of the largest inter-change freight yards in the nation. Owned and operated by the Soo Line and eight other railroads, Minnesota Transfer has 150 miles of trackage in its 13-mile area. Choice industrial sites are still available nearby—for information write R. S. Claar, Soo Line Railroad, Minneapolis 2.

So ship *SOO* if you ship to or thru
THE UPPER MIDWEST

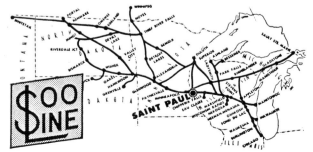

SOO LINE

—your working partner 7 days a week

35 1951

Above: It's August 1933 and the Minnesota State fair promoters at St. Paul have staged one of the dumbest stunts ever – a head on collision starring two tired Soo Standard 4-4-0's, **30** and **34**.

Robert Graham, L.M. Berger Collection

Right: The shameful and tragic mess in front of the grandstand on September 8, 1933.

Soo Line Railroad Collection

Below: April 1948 **2719**, an H-23 Pacific at the St. Paul Coaling Tower. This engine had undergone modernization and several upgradings, a steel cab, stoker, and other 'advancements,' as well as a larger tender. It was donated to the city of Eau Claire, Wisconsin.

Richard Hanschka Collection

Coal
Docks
and
Coaling

The first Rhode Island 4-4-0 engines were purchased as wood burners in 1885. Shortly thereafter the young road was to standardize on eastern soft coal as an energy source. Soo Line steam never did use crude bunker C fuel oil as used on many western roads. Coal was transported from Great Lakes ports to coaling docks most often by box-cars where it was shoveled off by hand. The coal dock operator would then load individual buckets with a shovel. A hoist or winch would lift the hinged buckets to tender height and then the bucket would be swung out and dumped. After 1912-1915, the typical coaling derrick was powered by air from the locomotive's air pump. It required some time to break the air line and then pump up the air pressure again. In order that passenger trains could stay on schedule, an auxiliary gas engine would be started in the derrick room for winching coal into those tenders.

Coal was delivered to the coal docks with their attached derrick sheds usually by boxcar. Originally, these sheds had capacities of 300 to 800 ton. Later, however, these were downsized and the derrickmen would shovel directly from the boxcars to load the lorry or buckets.

Larger terminals would have a coaling station or coaling tower of the McHenry or Fairbanks Morse type which had elevators to lift the coal up to a bin which was later dumped into tenders. Such coaling towers could receive their coal from a hopper car and were less labor intensive.

Lignite coal burned somewhat more rapidly and required a wider firebox grate and a greater draft in order to realize the same delivered energy to the boiler. Except for the engines delivered to the Bismarck, Washburn and Great Falls Railway, no Soo engines were so equipped to burn lignite from North Dakota.

William Egan, Jr. collection

William Egan and the Henning,MN coal dock in 1929. This was a two story dock. Barely visible behind the air driven gear winch was a smaller (pony) winch powered by a small water-cooled gas engine. The empty coal buckets were winched up to the storage shelf seen on the two upper shelves. When actually loading coal into tenders, the larger winch was used except when a passenger engine tender was being refueled. Because of schedule constraints, the gas powered unit was used so that the train could leave immediately - not having to wait for the locomotive's air pump to regain the lost air pressure.

Obviously, the larger and more powerful steam engines consumed considerably more coal and when stokers became available, the Soo installed stokers on those engines.

Soft coal for locomotive firing was purchased through a variety of outlets including the Clarkson Coal and Dock Company of St. Paul, the Pittsburg Coal Company and the Pittsburg Thin Vein Company. Coal was received via Great Lakes boats at Duluth, Ashland, Gladstone and Milwaukee as well by barge to St. Paul. During the second decade, the Soo paid between $2.75 and $2.90 a ton at the lake ports.

As expected, small 0-6-0 switch engines such as the class B-4 had very limited coal and water capacity (5000 gallons and 8 tons). Grate area on these engines was about 31 sq.ft. A small road passenger engine such as an H-1 light Pacific had a 44 sq. ft. grate area and carried 10 tons coal. Likewise, small freight engines

Above: Thief River Falls in 1906. The single pocket McHenry Coal dock included a 1000 ton storage shed and a trestle.

Stuart Nelson Collection

SPECIAL LOW
ROUND TRIP
TOURIST FARES
via

SOO LINE

TO RESORTS IN THE
CANADIAN ROCKIES
TICKETS ON SALE
DAILY
June 1st to September 30th, 1912

Ask for
Mountain Trips for Busy People

Stuart Nelson

Above: 1954—very little has changed at the engine terminal during the preceeding 48 years. Yes, the sand tower is new, diesel fueling has become almost the rule, and the round house doors are closing, but the big changes are yet to come.

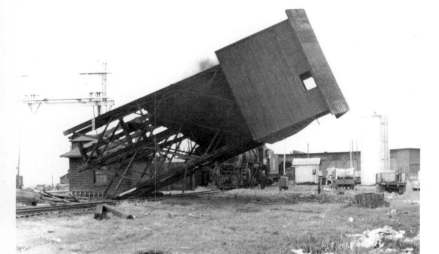

May 5, 1957: Down goes the tower with dynamite charges under two legs—51 years of service and a million memories. Just behind the falling tower is display engine 1024. To the right is a new diesel fuel vertical tank.

Stuart Nelson

such as the classes F-8, F-9 and F-10 Consolidations had tenders of about the same capacity with grate areas of about 47 sq. ft.

The class L-1 Mikes carried over 17 tons coal along with 12,000 gallons of water in their tenders. These engines and tenders weighed 513,600 lbs in working order and had a tractive power of 53940 lbs. They had a grate area of 63 sq. ft. The L-1 was geared for freight service with its 63 inch drivers. Some heavy passenger engines such as the Class H-23 Pacifics with 75 inch drivers also carried 17 & 1/2 tons coal. These stoker equipped steamers had a grate area of 52.75 sq. ft.

As engines and tenders became larger and taller, it became necessary to extend the height of the coal dock as well as the height and reach of the air winches in the derrick houses

Mountain type N-20 tenders carried 18,000 gallons along with 22 tons of coal. The grate area of an N-20 was 70 sq. ft. and their tractive power (with the booster) was 63,900 lbs. with a weight (engine and tender) in working order of 673,000 lbs. Just compare this to the original Standard 4-4-0 engines delivered to the Minneapolis and Pacific in 1887. These weighed (engine and tender with water and coal) 200,400 lbs., had a grate area of 15.8 sq.ft. and a tractive power of but 14,037 lbs.

The Soo Line purchased lignite coal from North Dakota mines to heat its depots and trackside buildings. Much of this coal came from the Burlington area just north west of Minot.

The Shoreham Coal Dock

R. Vierkanz photo, Pete Bonesteel Collection

Note the water hose and dozens of small details with the large tower at Shoreham.

Pete Bonesteel Collection

The Shoreham coal tower was able to service tenders with coal from both sides as these two photos by Robert Vierkanz document.

Kensal, ND, like South Haven, was a small town with a large McHenry type tower with seventeen bents supporting the tower. It had one pocket. For many years, Kensal was also favored with two water towers, the first having been built in 1893 and the second in 1910.

Soo Line Railroad

### *COALING FACILITIES,* Soo Line Railroad: West of Shoreham			
		Courtesy of S.J. Nelson	
Shoreham	McHenry 50 ton 2 pockets 1900-1958	Garrison	Derrick House ----
Buffalo	Derrick House 1886-	Max	Derrick House 1907-burned 1918 replaced-1954
South Haven	McHenry 50 ton 2 pockets 1904-1955	Plaza	Derrick House 1907-1939
Eden Valley	Derrick House 1886-	Sanish	Derrick House 1915-1953
Sedan	Derrick House 1886-	Henning	Derrick House 1904-1955
Glenwood	McHenry 50 ton 1 pocket 1905, additional pocket 1908 -1955	Detroit Lakes	Derrick House 1904-1940
		Mahnomen	Derrick House 1904-1937 Fairbanks-Morse 50 ton Coal Chute 1937-1955
Lowry	Derrick House 1887-		
Hoffman	Derrick House 1886-1955	Plummer	Derrick House 1904-1944 moved to Lake Bronson
Smiths Tank (Elliott)	Derrick House 1887-		
Fairmount	Derrick House -----	Thief River Falls	McHenry 50 ton 1 pocket 1905-1957
Hankinson	McHenry 50 ton 2 pockets 1907-	Karlstad	Derrick House 1904-1944
Enderlin	McHenry 50 ton 1 pocket 1905-1955	Lake Bronson	Derrick House 1944-1955
		Sultan-Noyes	Derrick House 1904-
Valley City	Derrick House 1893-	Oslo	Derrick House 1908-1955
Kensal	Derrick House 1893-1905 McHenry 50 ton 1 pocket 1905-1955	Fordville	Derrick House 1912-1955
		Adams	Derrick House 1905-1952
		Egeland	Derrick House 1905-1952
Harvey	Derrick House 1893-1955	Overly	Derrick House 1906-1952
Drake	Derrick House 1906-1955	Eckman	Derrick House 1906-1953
Voltaire	Derrick House 1927-1955	Devils Lake	Derrick House 1945-1954
Velva	Derrick House 1907-1927 moved to Voltaire	Darby	Derrick House 1912-1945 moved to Devils Lake
Minot	Coaling Platform 1914-1954	Holdingford	Derrick House 1908-1955
		Onamia	Derrick House 1908-1955
Donnybrook	Derrick House 1894-1906 moved to Flaxton	Moose Lake	Derrick House 1907-1910 McHenry 50-ton 1 pocket 1909-1956
Kenmare	Derrick House 1905-1955		
Flaxton	Derrick House 1906-1929	Superior (21st Street)	McHenry 50 ton 2 pockets 1909-1955
Portal	Derrick House 1893-replaced 1925-1955	Duluth	McHenry 50 ton 1 pocket 1910-1955
Imperial	Derrick House1906-1928	Iron Hub	Derrick House 1910-
Fortuna	Derrick House 1914-1955	Ironton	NP facility
Outlook	Derrick House 1914-1955	Palisade	Derrick House 1910-1955
Veblen	Derrick House 1915-1955	Federal Dam	Derrick House 1910-1955
Grenville	Coaling Platform 1917-1955	Scribner	Derrick House 1911-1955
		Osceola	Derrick House 1888-1896 moved to Amery Fairbanks-Morse Coal Chute 1945-1960
Lidgerwood	Coaling Platform 1887-		
Ransom	Derrick House 1887-1928 moved to Sanish	Dresser	
Oakes	Derrick House 1887-1955	St. Croix Falls	Coaling Platform 1887-
Kulm	Derrick House 1898-1955	Luck	Derrick House 1911-1945
Wishek	Derrick House 1901-1955	Frederic	Derrick House 1902-1913
Pollock	Derrick House 1901-1955	Markville	Derrick House 1912-1955
Napoleon	Derrick House 1901-1955		
Bismarck	Derrick House 1902-1955		
Wilton	Derrick House 1901-1940		
Underwood	Derrick House 1903-burned 1923 replaced-1955		

801, a J series Prairie takes on coal at Wishek in 1946. Note how the arm swings out from the coal dock and virtually the entire bottom of the bucket is hinged to dump the coal.

Wallace Pfeiffer

Wheat Line disaster ca. 1913. **172** -the last built of the D-2 Moguls loses its tender and coal. The section hands with their 'safety last' speeder have arrived to help out.

Percy Lamb collection

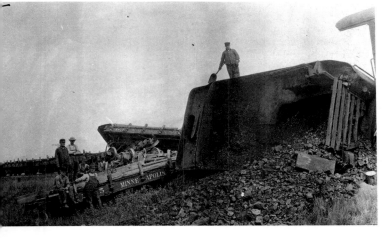

Not all coal found its way onto a tender hopper. Here, the section men at Baker (on the Drake line) haul coal by wheelbarrow to the depot in 1953. Virtually all Soo depots were kept warm with a coal fired furnace. The Soo purchased much North Dakota Lignite for heating use from the Burlington area just northwest of Minot.

From a color slide by Byron Knutson

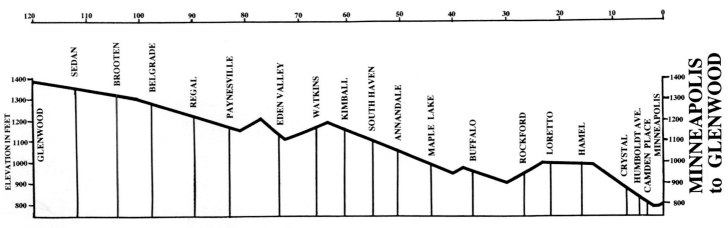

It's snowplow time in January 1975 with a Russell plow, an F unit covered wagon, a geep, and the mandatory caboose headed west from Minneapolis to the battle station in the 'white yonder.'

Soo Line Railroad

Left: Horsedrawn hack at Rockford after the new second class Soo Standard design had replaced the old Minneapolis and Pacific 20' wide depot. Note also the wrap-around platform with cream cans about to be loaded.

Ron Olin Collection

Right: 1912 postcard view of the Enderlin local or Dakota Express over the Crow river. Like so many of the local mills, this one succumbed to the efficiency of large companies like Pillsbury and Washburn-Crosby (which became the present day General Mills).

Pete Bonesteel Collection

The Minneapolis and Pacific

The Minneapolis and Pacific Railway was chartered in 1884 and absorbed into the Minneapolis St. Paul and Sault Ste. Marie Railway in the consolidation of 1888. During 1886-87 the line built westward from Minneapolis to Dakota Territory. Its purpose was to give Minneapolis milling interests a source of hard spring wheat independent of Jim Hill's Great Northern. A concise description of the M. and P. appears in *Part I* pp 15-17. The purpose of this section is to give pictorial coverage of the line to Glenwood and west to Hankinson.

It is impossible to give detailed descriptions of each town and hamlet in the space available so we will concentrate on a few selected communities realizing that the full story of the Minneapolis and Pacific can never be set down in the pages of even dozens of books.

Proceeding west from Shoreham to the Humboldt yard, the tracks of the Minneapolis and Pacific (now the Paynesville Sub) cross the old Great Northern diamond at Crystal on to Hamel and Rockford and over the Crow River. Buffalo, in Wright County, has in recent years become a bedroom community for Minneapolis. The story of the Buffalo depots is chronicled on page 109 *Part I*. Starting near Buffalo, and continuing beyond Elbow Lake, the countryside is dotted with lakes, large and small. Just to the west of South Haven, a substantial steel bridge carries rails over the Clearwater River. This river has its origin at Clear Lake situated in an upland till plain to the south in Meeker County. Soo tracks gently climb from the river to the plain at Kimball. These hills have been exploited for winter skiing much as the lakes provide for water skiing in warm months.

Eighty-two miles west from Minneapolis is Paynesville, a lake country town having 2200 inhabitants in 1990. Platted in 1887, the M.&P. had arrived in 1886 and built the 24' x 64' single story depot which was expanded in 1902, 1908, and 1911 to a final dimension of 24' x 127'

North American Creameries, described in following pages, had its start in Paynesville in 1901 when Frank Noonan established his first creamery and cold storage plant. The North American trade was important enough to the Soo such that in 1916 the original station platform was replaced with a 12' x 397' concrete platform.

Eden Valley waits for the Eastbound local (1890).

Paynesville Museum

Loretto Station–one of the original Minneapolis and Pacific stations–20' wide with a water tank in the background.

Ron Olin Collection

South Haven, 1912. Note a McHenry coal tower rather than a coal dock was here throughout the steam era.

Ed. Wertheim Collection

Here the Soo had a standard three pen stockyards (64' x 96') and a 60 foot turntable (constructed in 1898). At one time there was a single stall engine house.

Periodically, the North American Creamery at Paynesville would receive several carloads of new cream cans either as replacements or for expansion. The photo at left - taken around 1920 shows the dramatic overload on the station platform.

Paynesville Museum

Herb Stanton photo, James Welton Collection

Above: It is 1935 and steam is still king this frosty January morning as L-1 Mikado **1001** chugs west with whistle blowing and the North wind diverting that magnificient plume. L-1 is run on 63" drivers.

Left: Fun time at the fourth of July parade in Paynesville. An incredible output of butter for a tiny town combine with cream cans and egg crates to make for a most impressive display.

Paynesville Museum

Sad times, right: July 13, 1950, Number 26 time freight with AA FA Alco's crashed head on into extra 4001 west - an extra movement passenger train. Seventeen were injured including John Jaros, the engineer who stuck to his engine.

Richard Anderson

45

The original North American Creamery and cold storage plant at Paynesville was built in 1901. Photo from circa 1915.

Paynesville Historical Society

North American Creameries

Frank Noonan then moved to Alexandria and built a home not far from the Soo tracks and the North American plant. Adjacent to his home was an elaborate semi-formal park called "A little bit o Heaven."

By the time of Noonan's death in 1920, plants were also in operation in Oakes (North Dakota), and Watertown (South Dakota). His two sons took over the business and the product line grew such that by 1940 the following were produced or handled:

> Butter, tub, print and packaged
> Eggs, fresh, candled and canned (frozen)
> buttermilk processed and powdered
> cottage cheese
> poultry-turkeys, geese and ducks
> ice cream; manufactured at the
> Paynesville plant and marketed as "North
> American Ice Cream"
> Cold Shot- a pecan flavored confection
> miscellaneous frozen confections
> bottled spring and distilled water
> casein milk by product

The company was also a distributor for beer, tobacco, candy and fountain supplies.

Although North American Creameries were not the only milk, cream and egg operation on the Soo Line, this company was by far the largest with locations at Paynesville, Alexandria, Oakes and Carrington on the Soo as well as a plant in Watertown, South Dakota.

In the peak years of 1922-45, cream, milk and eggs were brought to these five plants from nearly 800 buying stations in the upper midwest and Montana.

Frank Noonan, the son of a carriage builder from St. Augustine, Illinois came to Paynesville (on the original main line of the Minneapolis and Pacific) in 1901 and established a modest creamery which along with its expansion to other sites was employing over a thousand men and women by the time of his death in September 1920.

Previous to moving to Paynesville, Noonan had had experience with cold storage and so he was a pioneer in the purchase of eggs and cream to churn butter during the abundant summer months when produce prices were low and with cold storage was able to hold the perishables to sell during scarcer times at higher prices.

Soon the Paynesville plant was at full capacity and a cold storage plant was erected at Alexandria. In those times cold storage meant using ice from nearby lakes to keep a large and well insulated building cool the entire summer by direct and evaporative cooling. Business boomed and on October 3, 1907 the Alexandria Citizen reported that North American was constructing a 36' x 100' creamery addition to its facility there to churn butter. The operation continued to prosper and provide employment for many, both on a permanent basis as well as seasonal.

Paynesville Historical Society

Ice was harvested at nearby Lake Koronis, hauled by horse and packed in the plant with sawdust from basement to roof to provide cooling for the season.

Gordon Twedt Collection

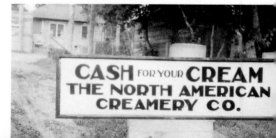

CASH FOR YOUR CREAM
THE NORTH AMERICAN
CREAMERY CO.

The Carrington Creamery in the early 1930's. It was torn down in 1992, having stood south of the track just adjacent to U.S. Highway 52. The original North American operation started in a wooden warehouse on the north side of Soo Line tracks. It dealt in eggs and was also a cream buying station for the other established plants. When constructed in 1927-28, it was the last of the five creamery plants to go into operation.

Foster County Historical Society

The creamery in Carrington was the last large expansion. Work was started on the building in 1927 and the plant was in full operation by 1928. World War II were real boom years for all the plants as the need for canned turkeys, dried milk and canned and dried milk for the military was acute. These years of plenty were followed by the fifties and financial reverses; most of the buying stations in western Minnesota and the Dakotas were turned over to the Fairmont Creamery of Moorhead. Eventually, one by one, the plants were sold off. The Carrington plant was sold to eight local employees who ran it profitably until 1970 when it was sold to a competitor who shortly thereafter discontinued operations. The Paynesville plant was sold to the Alstrom brothers who in turn sold out to AMPI— the big milk producers cooperative. AMPI continued to dry milk and make cheese in Paynesville. The Oakes

plant was also sold and eventually resold to Land o' Lakes cooperative.

A word or two about some of their operations is in order - - Milk from as far west as Montana would arrive at the Alexandria or Paynesville plants- completely fermented. Spills in the baggage cars would smell of rotten milk during the warm summer months. The concept of 'renovated butter' deserves mention since the Paynesville plant was one of only two in Minnesota licensed to do this. Prior to mechanical refrigeration, a great deal of home churned butter was made on local farms. The quality of this butter was poor and the Paynesville plant was equipped to melt down the butter, mix it with milk and then rechurn it. Such finished product was packed in 60 pound tubs specially marked and sold for commercial use in bakeries and restaurants. Some was 'printed' and sold to consumers as grade B 'renovated' butter.

It's In The Bag

The successful farmer is the one who realizes that vitamin and mineral enriched feed makes healthier, sturdier animals — animals that mean greater profits and productivity for the farm.

For the UPPER MIDWEST It's—

Arvilla Feeds

CHICK SCRATCH   LAYING MASH—Reg. and Pellets
CHICK STARTER & BUILDER   CALF MEAL
    Regular and Pellets
DAIRY FEEDS   18% HOG CONCENTRATE

BRING YOUR EGGS HERE   **NORTH AMERICAN CREAMERIES, INC.**   YOUR BEST EGG MARKET

The fleet of trucks from 1931 shown above at the Carrington plant was typical. North American had over 100 buying stations in various towns and cities throughout Minnesota, the Dakotas, and Montana. The trucks would carry butter, milk products, ice cream, and pop to retail outlets in the area and return with eggs, farm-made butter, and cream from the buying stations for processing.

Foster County Historical Society

You Can't Go Wrong on This Combination

Produce—Quality Cream—and bring it in often.

You will find that the little extra labor required to produce FIRST GRADE CREAM, and deliver it frequently, will be more than repaid in INCREASED INCOME. Cream that is handled in clean utensils, cooled after skimming, and sold promptly makes BETTER BUTTER.

Paying today: No. 1 Cream 49c
                  Sweet Cream 52c

We are on the job every working day in the year, ready to take care of your CREAM, EGGS and POULTRY.

Remember there is no substitute for good butter. You will like our "Pv Quality" Creamery butter, made from local sweet cream. Satisfaction or your money back.

NORTH AMERICAN CREAMERY COMPANY

"Your logical Market"

"We never let the sun go down on a can of cream unpaid for."

OCTOBER 1928

North AMERICAN STORAGE COMPANY
Alexandria, Minn

1907 View of the Alexandria cold storage plant with creamery. The design is similar to the Paynesville plant, and made from native brick produced at the Miltona brickyard.

Douglas County Museum

The Oakes (North Dakota) creamery. Eggs were handled here, candled and shipped to New York and Philadelphia markets in 30 dozen cases, as well as canned and frozen.

Ethel Bassler Cox photo

Building westward in 1886, the Minneapolis and Pacific reached Belgrade and Brooten. The latter town was the junction of the cutoff line to Superior - Duluth. Constructed through farmland, and thereafter swamp and forest, the Brooten line served as an important bypass for western grain travelling to the Duluth inland seaport.

Pete Bonesteel Collection

May 29, 1911. The Belgrade depot is somewhat an anomaly along the old M. and P. Note the short two-story center section spliced with waiting room and freight rooms on opposite ends. Note the new grain elevator (of cribbed construction) under construction to the left.

Paynesville Museum

Construction train from the 1890's tied up at Paynesville. Note the link-pin couplers. The living quarters atop the flat cars later became portable depots or maintenance structures.

1939 - 1940

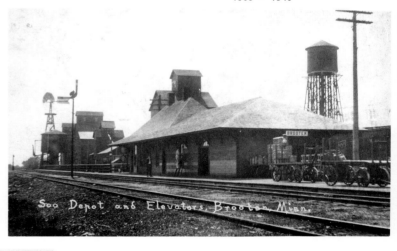

To the right is the newer Soo Line depot at Brooten, a typical one-story first class design which replaced the original Minneapolis and Pacific 20' wide structure. The view below from Pete Bonesteel's collection is from 1915.

Pete Bonesteel Collection

Brooten is 104 miles west from Minneapolis and the branch point for the Soo's line to Moose Lake and Duluth Superior. (Constructed 1907-1909)

Paynesville Museum Collection

1947 Air view of Glenwood, around noon with #106 arriving.

Gently rolling fertile farmland describes the landscape east of Glenwood which is at an elevation of 1420 feet. This picturesque and onetime very important junction point and terminal town is nestled in the ice - block basin on the shores of long and lovely Lake Minnewaska. During 1886 the fledgling M. and P. constructed some nine miles further west to Lowry. The Northern Pacific had reached Glenwood earlier, but following 1887-1888 when the railroad decided to have its terminal here, Glenwood became a Soo Line town.

Glenwood proper is built in the valley adjacent to the lake. Soo tracks, however, are on the 'hill' to the north of the business district. This area of the city is called 'Soo Hill.' 1903 saw the fifteen year old Minneapolis, St.Paul and Sault Ste. Marie Railway going north from Glenwood. By 1904 it had reached north to Winnipeg (actually Noyes). Thus the yards, shops and roundhouse were expanded - 6 stalls were added making the roundhouse a very functional 20 stalls.

During 1909, the expanded terminal was seeing 35 trains a day originate or pass. 'Soo Hill' had four grain elevators besides warehouses for four separate breweries. At that time not only was the 20 stall roundhouse in operation, but also a 50' x 100' boiler house with three boilers, a water treatment plant, a sand house, a supply house, an oil house, two coal chutes with 50 ton capacity each and a wheat inspection department. Besides all this there were over 40 men working in the roundhouse alone and the Soo maintained the necessary 'luxury' of keeping two extra road engines here as spares for emergencies.

By 1949, employment had dropped to 87 on the payroll. This slowly declined as dieselization engulfed the Soo. Even so, during 1985 there were still nearly 70 on the payroll - a figure which had dropped to 50 by the time yard operations were closed in 1987.

The Pope County Museum on the shores of Lake Minnewaska has excellent files of old newspapers as well as impressive interpretive displays of area history including that of the Native Americans.

Glenwood was platted in 1866 and incorporated in 1881. Little Falls and Dakota Railroad built through here in 1882 - four years before the Minneapolis and Pacific came west, but Glenwood quickly became a Soo town with its shops, roundhouse and division point. The Northern Pacific purchased the Little Falls and Dakota in 1900.

Ron Olin Collection

It is October 1972 - five years after the discontinuation of the Winnipegger. For many years, the Soo Line had been double-tracked over the underpass for the waiting passenger train to the west of the depot. With the holding track no longer in use it was removed along with the steel girder bridge.

Pope County Musuem

Nine miles west of Glenwood and some 130 miles west from Minneapolis is Lowry, named after Thomas Lowry. Lowry was the father of the Minneapolis - St.Paul Streetcar System and an early booster of the Soo; he was president of the Soo during two separate terms. A brief history of his career is found on page 204, *Part I*. Lowry, Minnesota became the western terminus of the M. and P. in 1886 and an eight stall round house was constructed here. Its glory was brief for, as noted previously, Glenwood quickly became the dominant Soo community.

Kensington is the home of the much discussed and maligned 'Kensington Runestone' This stone was found nearby in a farmer's field in 1898. It has runic writing telling of eight Swedes and twenty two Norwegians who had traveled by boat and overland in 1362 from *Vinland* (Newfoundland). Since it has never been authenticated or disproven - the story it tells will never be known in full. It now rests in a museum in downtown Alexandria.

No. 5 waits at Glenwood while the engine crew discusses a problem with the master mechanic: 1949.

Gerald Wodarz

Barrett

John Cartwright Drawing

It would be amiss not to tell how the Union Cemetery northwest of Barrett came in to existence. In 1892, a westbound passenger train jumped the track upon crossing the Pomme de Terre River a mile east of Barrett. After the wreck was cleared and the injured carried to help, the dead were slowly identified. Six dead men could not be identified and when their bodies were never claimed - the Soo offered the village of Barrett land for a cemetery if the villagers would bury the six victims. These unknown six still rest with the remains of many other departed souls in Union Cemetery today. Barrett was platted May 7, 1887 and was named after General Barrett, a Civil War veteran who farmed west near Herman. A second tragedy struck Barrett on the morning of May 1, 1900 when the entire main street business section burned down. The town rebuilt, this time with a wider main street illuminated with gas lights. Barrett continues to be a cultural stronghold in the 1990's with the Prairie Wind Players performing in historic Roosevelt Hall. The Prairie Fire Children's Theatre also makes Barrett its home.

All railroads needed and used ice for cooling, both for reefer cars that hauled perishables, as well as for cooling air conditioning bunkers in passenger cars (few of the Soo Line's passenger fleet had mechanized air conditioning).

Starting in 1894, the Soo Line obtained its ice by purchase from Hjelle Ice Works on the shores of spring-fed Lake Barrett.

Ole Hjelle designed the incline which elevated the ice from the lake to the platform at track side for loading into the box cars as pictured on these pages.

Grant County Museum

Troop train picking up WWI draftees going to training camp, Barrett 1918.

Barrett Main Street, looking northwest. Note the dirt street, and the blacksmith (the L shaped building at the lower right) with wagons tied to hitching posts on main street. The tank, depot and Lake Barrett are to the right. Circa 1915.

Originally, the ice was pulled up the incline by horses to the platform, but by the turn of the century, a steam engine powered the elevator as shown in the 1905 photo. Eventually, the operation was powered by a couple of one-cylinder Fairbanks Morse Semi diesel engines. Weeds were cut in the lake in the fall of the year to assure that the ice would be crystal-clear when the lake froze over.

The Hjelles: Ole, sons Elmer, Oscar, Norman, and Clifford, and later, grandson Tom Hjelle, were to operate the plant from 1894 to 1932, and again from 1943 until it closed after the 1972-73 season. In 1946, the E.W. Wylie company leased the plant and later purchased it from the Hjelles, although the Hjelles and local labor continued to perform the actual work.

From 1932 until 1943, ice for the Soo Line was harvested by another company (at Forada) on the Winnipeg line near Alexandria.

During the early 1950's, the Soo used about 50,000 tons of ice yearly, of which 30,000 tons was harvested at Barrett. In 1951, 756 box cars of ice were taken from Lake Barrett as far west as Whitetail, but also east to Weyerhauser and Rhinelander.

Soo ice houses filled with Barrett Lake of varying capacities were located at:

Shoreham	Mahnomen
St. Paul	Federal Dam
Thief River Falls	Fordville
Glenwood	Sanish
Hankinson	Bismarck
Harvey	Kenmore
Enderlin	Flaxton
Portal	Whitetail
Rhinelander	

The Soo's ice houses at Duluth, Superior, Ashland, Sault, St. Marie, Steven's Point and Ford du Lac were all filled with local ice from area lakes.

During the 1959-60 season, 422 carloads of ice were harvested in 12 days. By 1969-70, 200 carloads, 123 carloads in 1970-71, and after the 72-73 harvest, the operation was entirely discontinued. By this time, the Soo, and the Canadian Pacific had enough mechanical reefers for perishable haulage. It should be mentioned, that through the years there were dozens of other ice contractors for the Soo Line–some even owned their own ice houses on the railroad.

Richard Yaremko

Reds, whites and blacks-5250 diesel horses penetrate eastward through a rolling burnt orange prairie near Barrett. Sept. 13, 1978. Drought conditions were common throughout much of Minnesota and the Dakotas that year.

Left: Minnesota State Highway 55 parallels the Soo main west from Minneapolis. Oftentimes the highway flows right near the main artery to North Dakota and Canada. Near Hoffman, Minn. Aug. 7, 1988.

Otto Dobnick

Grant County Historical Society

Elbow Lake, the county seat of Grant County, had the distinction of having a riot between the construction crew of the Minneapolis and Pacific with that of Jim Hill's Great Northern. The M.&P. reached Elbow Lake first and so it was up to the Great Northern to build the diamond. The Grant County Herald reported (10-21-1886) *"A riot among the railroad men at Elbow Lake --- called Sheriff Linden --- to the seat of war. The disturbance was all over --- but several men were severely injured in the fracas. --- The result of the row was the closing of the saloon and the removal of the stock of liquors to Ashby."*

Above: Elbow Lake, 1896. The original Minneapolis and Pacific depot was razed to make room for the memorable brick, tile, and stone structure of 1916.

Right: Work continued through the winter of 1916-17 on the distinctive brick depot at Elbow Lake. This general design was shared with West Duluth and Osceola Wisconsin.

Soo Line Photo, Stuart Nelson Collection

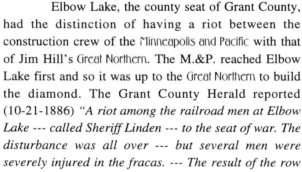

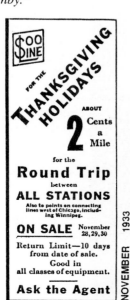

For the Minneapolis and Pacific the winter days of 1888 were marred by infrequent and simply inadequate service. Again the Grant County Herald (2-2-1888): *"That great competitor of the ox cart system of transportation, the Minneapolis [&] Pacific Railway sent a passenger train west of Lowry on Monday for the fifth time this year. The snow had melted off the road, the rails were perfectly dry, there was no side wind and the signal service had reported clear and calm weather for ten days. The officials deserve great praise for the bravery displayed in venturing to expose their infant to the rigors of a possible blizzard. As we go to press there is a cloud in the northwestern sky about the size of a man's hand, so look out for a report that the wonderful snowplow is broken again . The next train is likely to arrive one week from Monday."*

One of many Soo Line classics now gone forever —a victim of excess insurance and taxes to a railroad that today provides but wholesale transport services—razed during December, 1986.

Only four years had passed following its completion when the Elbow Lake depot was wounded badly by the wreck of November 17, 1920. Fortunately, the depot's recovery was complete.

Both photos: Grant County Historical Society

North Dakota

As the Minneapolis and Pacific Railway was pushing west during 1886, its sister road, the Minneapolis, Sault Ste. Marie and Atlantic Railway, was working its way eastward through Wisconsin forest and swamp towards the Sault and its connection with the Canadian Pacific. The 218 miles the M & P Railway completed during 1886 was truly a heroic effort. The end of the tracks for the winter of 86-87 was Lidgerwood, North Dakota–just at the southwestern edge of the famed Red River Valley. During 1887, the line was extended as far west as Boynton, North Dakota. At that time there was scattered settlement all along the line—enough to ensure wheat for the Minneapolis mills (which by then were in a constant state of expanding capacity - roller mills and the middlings purifier had been introduced earlier). This was an era when midwestern wheat and Minneapolis flour in particular were rapidly developing markets not only on the east coast but in Europe as well.

The year 1888 brought the consolidation of the four previously chartered railways into the Minneapolis, St. Paul and Sault Ste. Marie Railway with the financial backing and assurance of the Canadian Pacific. Thus was to start the 'golden age' of expansion of the Soo. In the spring of 1891, grading, ties and rail started northwesterly from Hankinson sometimes across virgin territory to open up central North Dakota - crossing the Northern Pacific at Valley City and the Great Northern at Minot. The Soo was to reach Wyndmere in the Red River Valley and Enderlin along the Maple River during 1891. It crossed the Sheyenne River at Valley City, and the James River near Kensal, into the rich farm country of Foster County and Carrington. The line continued into Harvey (where a second Division Point was established) across the Wintering River near Balfour. It thereafter advanced towards Minot in the Mouse River Valley. From Minot the Soo was forged up the Des Lacs valley to Kenmare and on to Portal in 1893 to establish the young line's second connection with the Canadian Pacific.

By 1897 there were 100 line elevators on the Soo in North Dakota. Most belonged to the Minneapolis firms of Osborne & McMillan and the Atlantic Elevator Company, although the Royal Elevator Company owned eleven along Soo tracks that year. The majority of elevators in those days were of 20,000 bushel capacity or less. As the years passed, the number of elevators and their capacities increased to match the expanding settlement of the state. The twentieth century brought more scientific agriculture and by the 1960s, yields were increasing rapidly, not only for wheat and barley, but also for new crops like potatoes, sunflowers and sugar beets. The discovery of vast underground deposits in Canada of potash fertilizer led to unit trains of this valuable commodity moving eastward through the Portal gateway. With deregulation the railroads were at last able to competitively price haulage and unit grain trains of 52 cars became the norm. Only the larger and well managed elevators were able to grade, clean, process and load these unit trains efficiently. Thus the size of elevators gradually grew and numbers dwindled. Many of today's elevators are farmers' cooperatives; the Soo has helped with their marketing not only by lengthening house tracks and elevator sidings, but also by leasing and purchasing ever increasing numbers of covered hoppers for grain lading.

Hankinson

Eastbound local No. 6 stops at Hankinson to take on coal. Note that Engineer Colnell Gossman has the canvas rolled back behind him and is ready to roll.

Note the small water tank. The Soo did not have its own well, thus this tank was filled with city water.

Both photos by Wodarz - Jim Fischer Collection

*Manual turntable at Hankinson with **13** Soo Standard on the balance.* Note the outhouse, also a Soo standard necessity.

Jim Fischer Collection

Hankinson's classic depot with the beanery nearest on the right. Note the single pocket McHenry coaling tower in the distance on the left.

Left: Interior of Hankinson beanery circa 1920. There probably was a special on oranges and bananas that week.

Both Photos: Jim Fischer Collection

Above: 1918 postcard view of the Hankinson four stall roundhouse. Note the supply of ties, cattle car, outhouse and lubricant shed.

Left: 1955 finds **368**, an Alco RSC-2 1500 hp road switcher refueling at the Hankinson round-house. The tank car on the left contains the diesel fuel and the Alco's air compressor is forcing the oil to flow to its fuel tanks.

Ken Soroos

Right: New GP-30's **709** and **717** leading an eastbound freighttrain near Hankinson during their first months of service in the Summer of 1963. Note that the winterization hatches haven't yet been installed.

Ken Soroos

After diesels took over on No. 5 / No. 6 (105/106), the Enderlin local stop at Hankinson was very brief. The Pacific class locomotives needed mandatory coal and water stop here.

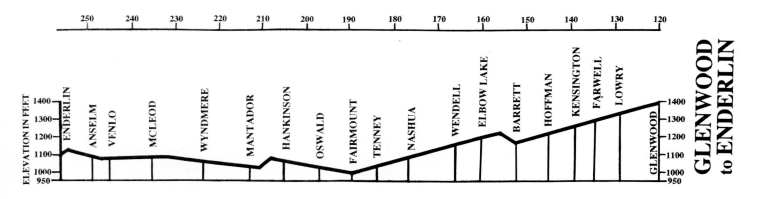

It's a mid morning early spring day and **701** hurries No. 6 eastbound Enderlin local between Wyndmere and Matador.

Gerald Wodarz

Early depots were often 12 feet wide by 24 or 30 feet in length. They were originally crew housing on flat cars of the construction trains. After these 'shacks' were replaced by more standard depot designs, these same structures showed up track side as coal sheds or tool houses.

State Historical Society of Wisconsin

Gerald Wodarz lived south of Wyndmere and had daily opportunities to record Soo movements from his farmyard vantage point. Perhaps my favorite of his many classic prints is the prairie local in 1950.

Enderlin

Soo survey crews reached Enderlin in 1890 and rails reached this hilly picturesque town in October 1891. The town's plat was filed October 7, 1891. Perhaps headquarters felt the Maple River would be a good source of water for Soo iron horses. However; after settling in and putting in a turntable and building the first section of a roundhouse in 1892, the railroad found that the Enderlin water was bad, very bad. It foamed, which made steaming difficult. Initally, the railroad took the easy way out and set up a water tank over by Anselm on the banks of the Sheyenne River. Until 1913 little Enderlin water was used. After a water treatment plant was built in 1913, Enderlin as a division point came fully into its own.

Al Ohrt Collection

1911 Postcard view of the (in 1905) new depot (24' x 120')

Douglas Wick Collection

1935 view of main street in Enderlin. The depot is plain in view at the end. Note the simplicity of the ads and the honesty of the storefronts.

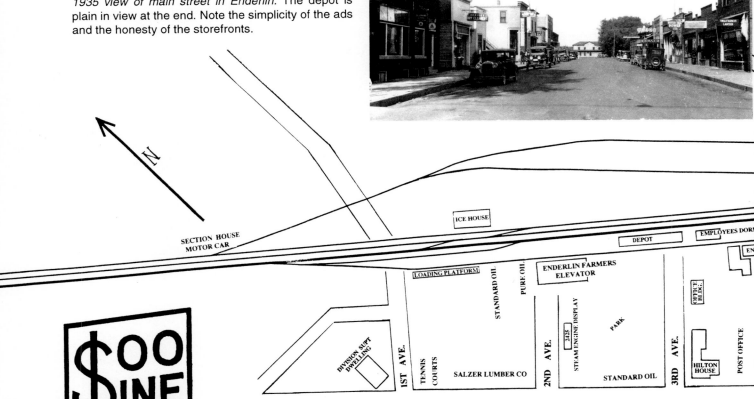

The roundhouse was enlarged in 1897, 1903 and finally in 1907 to 24 stalls. The 90 foot turntable was installed in 1919.

The original 1892 depot was destroyed by fire in 1905 and a new one was finished later that same year, The design of this 1905 depot was similar to the Bismarck depot constructed at about the same time (the latter being faced with brick) Please see page 106 *Part I*.

In 1893 a large railroad hotel was constructed - *the Hilton House* - and for many years this was managed by the Lasley Company which also ran the lunch room in a nearby concrete block building built in 1911. The 35' x 67' brick office building, pictured on page 91 *Part I*, was constructed in 1946 and remains in use today. Use of the 1905 depot was discontinued in 1972.

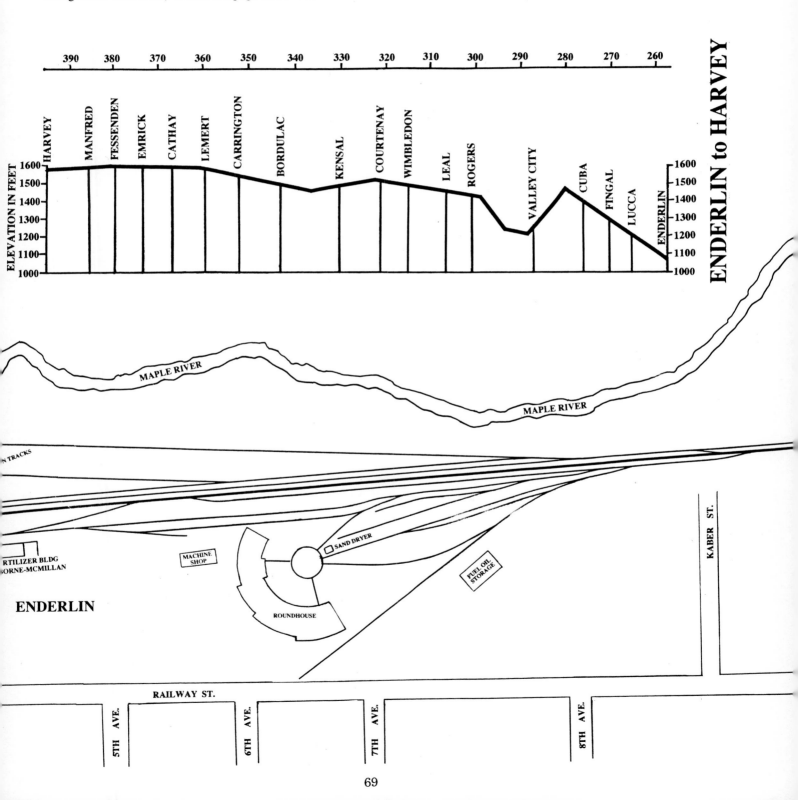

ENDERLIN to HARVEY

ENDERLIN

Olive Jankowski

East of Enderlin the No.105 (or No. 5) with heavy Pacific **737** on the point. 1949

William Flint

748, *an SD40* delivered to the Soo in 1970 takes on sand at the Enderlin yard.

Left: Enderlin May 26, 1970 during the flood of the Maple River. This view shows well the arrangement of the yard tracks, leads, roundhouse and shop. The depot and former beanery are along the tracks between the two elevator complexes.

Photo by Jennings for the Soo Line Railroad, Stuart Nelson Collection

By World War I the division had more than 200 employees in Enderlin. Besides the roundhouse, locomotive repair shop, a car shop, boiler house and a large ice house, here was found the second largest stockyards on the Soo with 96 pens.

It seems wrong that there might be a seedy side to this beautiful village, but then there was the strange suicide of the restaurant manager about 1941. Another incident of some notoriety occurred at the turn of the century when Fred Underwood sent out a fake organizer for the American Railway Union to test the 'loyalty' of the workers to the Soo management. Those employees caught signing up with the bogus organizer were fired.

A division point will have its heroes and engineer George Adams was just one of many legends back in the 1940's. Not only was he a poet whose poems were published in *Liberty* and other magazines (he wrote the famous *'Three Button Wonder' of the Soo*), but he was also a master of the locomotive and a rather sly 'bender of the rules.' Once he came into the office in Enderlin after tying up No. 3 (the west bound passenger) and said- "You need a new set of banjoes on the crossing at Nashua, the Great Northern was still a long way out and we were late." What he was saying was this: the railroad crossing between the main line of the Great Northern and the Soo Line was located just west of Nashua, MN. The GN had their plant wired further out for their trains than for the Soo trains. George was on a passenger train very closely approaching the crossing and the GN freight was just hitting the circuit about a mile and a half out. He was

moving faster than the GN but the signal arm (banjo) dropped across the Soo track and went RED. You guessed it --- George went right on through, beating the GN easily and safely and still not stopping the freight which had the green light on the Great Northern main line. This type of infarction truly occurred on more than just one occasion. Such infarctions were difficult for a dispatcher to explain to the superintendent. Just one other George Adams story for flavor - it seems he was a bit daring with running coal and water stops if he could make time. Once, while running west with a way freight, he ran out of coal ten miles east of Harvey. Rumor has it that a section crew had its pile of ties shrink considerably after George and his fireman helped themselves to make those last ten miles.

The 1973 view of the Enderlin depot shows that little changes were made during its 67 years of active use. An extension to the second floor was completed in the 1920's, and division offices were here until the 1946 building was finished. (See page 91 *Part I*)

Photo by Olive Jankowski

Cement block restaurant 25' x 65'- built in 1911 is still standing in 1994. It is currently being used as a trainmen's registerroom.

Enderlin Musuem Collection

Valley City is one of several substantial towns or cities served by the Soo which were settled as a result of an earlier railroad's presence, the Northern Pacific came here crossing the Sheyenne River in 1872 and the Soo trailed some twenty years later. A remarkable little electric interurban line 1.4 miles in length served to connect the Soo's depot north of Valley City with the NP depot downtown. The Valley City Street and Interurban Railway served the community from 1905 until September of 1953. The Soo's purchase of the electric line in 1953 enabled it to serve businesses along that line on the near north side. (see *Part I* pages 128-29)

The depot here, 24' x 113',was one of the Soo Standard second class designs with a larger than usual waiting room. It was notable for its 'clipped gables' on the ends of the roof. During the days of steam Valley City had a coaling station with derrick, 14 buckets and two lorries. Additional trackside structures included a standard wood tub water tower with a windmill, a steam pump and a special hydrant for water service to passenger trains besides the usual maintenance sheds and section house.

Valley City, comfortably nestled in the beautiful Sheyenne river valley, is the county seat of Barnes County and its 1990 population was 7,163. It is home to a state university and the North Dakota Winter Shows. It is also noted by rail fans as the location of the famed High Line Bridge carrying the tracks of the former Northern Pacific over the Sheyenne River. Kenmare and Valley City share the distinction of being some of the most picturesque communities along western Soo ways. Journeying to the northwest, Soo tracks skirt Bald Hill dam on the Sheyenne. This dam backs up Lake Ashtabula which is part of the Red River's flood control network and a fine place to fish in eastern North Dakota.

Hills forming the Sheyenne valley rise 200 feet or more above river level. In days of yore the Sheyenne was a huge river—today's terraces mark ancient levels at which the waters flowed. Going northwest from Valley City, the Soo grade is on one of these terraces and crosses under the Northern Pacific Hi Line Bridge which traverses the entire valley. During the closing of the glacial period the river carved deeply into the Cretaceous shales that form some of the present day valley walls.

Climbing from Valley City the tracks ascend a narrow and deep coulee to Rogers (elevation 1422). Here is a large and level prairie where the Soo crosses former Northern Pacific tracks. The shared depot at the Rogers diamond was of Soo construction.

At Rogers: a diamond carried the Soo's main over the former NP branch from Sanborn to McHenry in Foster county. McHenry was noteworthy among American branch line railroads in that a turning loop was used for reversing rather than the common turntable or 'wye.' BN trains now only come to Rogers from Sanborn: the Baldhill Dam and federal fish hatchery is just east of Rogers. The Rogers depot was a joint NP/Soo depot of Soo construction.

Ed. Wertheim Collection

At Valley City the Soo tracks remained east of the Sheyenne River along one of the valley ledges. The station was over a mile north of the downtown area. Note the double waiting room doors and the truncated ends of the depot gables.

Soo Line Railroad Collection

Soo passenger train about 1912 with the Hi Line bridge of the Northern Pacific to the North. The bridge is 3700 feet in length and 147 feet high.

Gary Anderson Collection

To the right: from 1905 until 1947, passengers detraining at Soo's (north) Valley City depot could travel to the downtown area or connect with the Northern Pacific low line main using the Valley City Street and Interurban Service. 1907 postcard view from the collection of Al Ohrt.

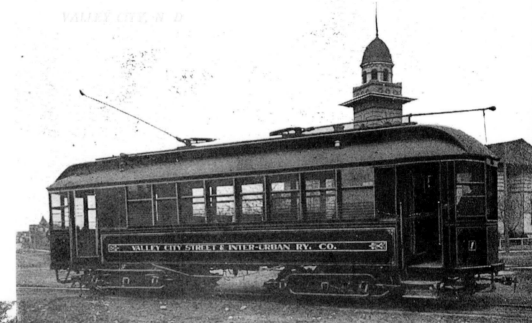

Al Ohrt Collection

Below: a late 1940's view of a northbound Soo freight train approaching the north line bridge.

Douglas Wick Collection

Stuart Nelson Collection

From 1947 until 1953 freight service continued over this tiny line using the motor car shown above. The Soo Line purchased the 1.4 mile short line in 1953, pulled down the wire and dieselized the service.

73

J. David Ingles

Soo and fifth can be found in dozens of communities spread throughout the upper midwest. Here in Kensal, 'Cat' powered **4301** drifts west—snowplow and all on this cloudy July day, 1991.

1910   **Pete Bonesteel Collection**

To the left: a more general view of the Kensal station. Of note are the two water towers in Kensal. The original one to the east was built in 1893, and the newer one in the foreground was built in 1910. A good number of Irish Americans settled here, and thus Kensal came to be named after county Cork Ireland.

**1919 Photo by Herb Stanton
(Jim Welton Collection)**

WIMBLEDON

This October 27, 1915 view of Wimbledon is simply remarkable.   **Wimbledon Historical Society**

Wimbledon, which had originally been named Gibson after one of the early settlers, was developed by the Soo in 1892 with the Minnesota Loan and Trust acting as agent. It was common practice for all western railroads to use a closely linked development company to lay out townsites and sell the lots during frontier times.

Wimbledon's first elevator was built late in 1892 and by 1899 some 900,000 bushels of grain were being marketed here annually. Such was the demand for grain markets in this area that eight elevators were up and running by 1908 at which time the village's population was over 600.

By 1913 the Midland Continental R.R. had reached its northern terminus at Wimbledon. It is of interest that Peggy Lee, a great pops singer from the 1940s, grew up in the Midland depot during the thirties where her father was the agent.

Wimbledon was named after the Borough of Wimbledon in London-now famous for its annual tennis tournaments. Although its 1990 census is but 275, it is still the second largest town in Barnes County (after Valley City).

Travelling west from Wimbledon on the Soo the landscape presents broad prairies with large boulders and a few shallow lakes east and west of Courtenay and over to Kensal in Stutsman county.

Kensal's 1990 census of 191 hardly pays tribute to the fact that this town was one of the main coaling stops along Soo's mainline through North Dakota. It is nestled in the Elysian Moraine of ancient Lake Agassiz. Travelling onward, the rails drop into the James River Valley with Arrow Wood Lake just south of the trestle bridge over James river. Moraine like hills can be seen rising to some 200 feet on either side of the tracks as we continue northwest. The line passes two small lakes to the north as we come into the rich farmlands of Foster county. Approaching Carrington the crew (and in former days the passengers) can see Hawk's Nest, a high preglacial pinnacle and a game hunter's paradise.

Wimbledon Historical Society

75

Jim Welton Collection

Facing Page: **A Moment in Time**

Soo Line **701**, a 4-6-2 Light Pacific slowly pulls away from the depot after a brief stop. A lone combo is all that is needed to service this run in the middle of Granger country. As the automobile becomes more popular, this local and all others in the Soo system will befcome obsolete. But that moment in time still brings back fond memories.

Painting by Larry Fisher

Bordulac is derived from the French for 'border of the lake' which refers to its location on the west shore of Lake George. The town was originally platted as Chihaun by the Soo in 1892, but the name was changed when a post office was established in 1895. This 1948 view of the depot shows the agent's bay knocked out by the passing snowplow.

1910 Bordulac   **Foster County Museum**

Al Ohrt Collection

Missed the engine, but caught the town! It seems as if elevators were more important than the engine (which looks like a tender to a 2-8-0). In 1910, Bordulac, N.D. had four elevators, and a landscape devoid of trees. The Soo brought the people to the town, and cars and trucks were to export them at milepost 343 west from Shoreham. The elevation here is 1530 feet.

CARRINGTON

SOO RY. STATION, CARRINGTON, N. DAK.

CHICAGO and MILWAUKEE
TO THE
PACIFIC COAST

ROUTE TO THE NORTH PACIFIC COAST

July 1900 postcard view of Standard 2nd Class depot Carrington (the county seat of Foster county). Unusual are the separate-end entrances for the mens' and ladies' waiting rooms. The sign on the left advertises Klondyke service; the sign on the right (under the Soo sign) advertises through cars to Boston.

Gordon Twedt Collection

SOO LINE DEPOT – 1955
CARRINGTON, N. D.

HD Connor, photo. Gordon Twedt Collection

November 1990: The end finally comes to Carrington's depot landmark. Note the propane tank; during the 'late depot era,' heating was no longer based on North Dakota lignite.   **Carrington Independent**

H A R V E Y

1909 postcard view by W. Olson of Harvey's 14-stall roundhouse and turntable. Note the modular track sections in the right foreground. This Wells County town of 2300 remains as the crew change point for the increasingly busy western main line of today's CP/Soo. Just 40 miles east is New Rockford, former division point on the Great Northern's Surry Cutoff which parallels Soo tracks for almost 170 miles.

Gordon Twedt

Gordon Twedt Collection

The twin water towers were Harvey's trademark. Water from the dammed pond, shown in the inset photo (collection of Russel Olsen), was pumped by the pumps in the low dark building.

Richard Yaremko

GP 7 382, GP 40 735 and 2 covered wagon F3 B units pull the tonnage east from the Dakota prairies towards Minnesota and its 10,000 plus lakes. Near Enderlin, September 13, 1978.

William Flint

Above: Eastbound leaves the Enderlin yard on the main on a cloudy, bright Dakota day in May, 1973.

Left: Curves, hills, dale and bridge. An Eastward Portal to Minneapolis hotshot snakes under the Burlington Northern's Hi Line bridge near Valley City.

Robert Kjelland

2403- a GP 9 originally delivered to the Wisconsin Central in 1954 with 50 foot double door box 15592 in tow. A very short train leaves the Harvey yard on September 5, 1977.

Richard Yaremko

William Flint

405–another GP 9 with its original high-hooded noses enters Harvey's turntable.

200A *at Baker, ND 1953:* The original F3 covered wagon from 1947 has already lost its B unit as it cruises the Drake line in search of grain.

Byron Knutson

Richard Yaremko

East(bound) meets West(bound) on the main at Voltaire. Soo **748** versus Soo **786** September 4, 1977.

Harvey Roundhouse and Double Water Towers.   **Leonard Drabus**

Looking East with the depot and overpass behind, our gaze quickly notes the peculiar existence of two water towers. The main line is to the left. Note also the canted upright supports on the towers; these were higher than standard. (1913)

Right: F-8 **440** consolidation is readied at Shoreham before delivery to Harvey for display on depot grounds. (June 1957)

Robert Vierkanz Photo: Pete Bonesteel Collection

Below: the Harvey roundhouse accident during the 1940's. **716** came in fast from the east while **450** was simultaneously spotting the coal dock. The switches were against **716** and it ran the switch and hit **450**. The tender broke loose from **450** and flipped over yielding the scene below.

Don Fisher

BALFOUR

Balfour had originally been proposed as a secondary terminal along mainline Soo - a distinction which went to Drake when water could not be found here in acceptable quantities.

The terminal lies in the drift region and the surface shows marks of the receding glacier of 10,000 years ago. There are long drum lines like minature morraines which run parallel to each other SE to NW and also parallel to the main line rails.

The altitude here is 1613 feet and in the early part of the century the town grew enthusiastically, having one of the early telephone systems in the state. Swedes and Russian-Germans settled here and by 1904, the community boasted two banks, six elevators, a hospital, three churches and a brick school house. The population was to peak at 399 in 1910.

Modern convienences came to Balfour with the introduction of electric lighting in 1914 (Even Governor Hanna came out from Bismarck to celebrate the dedication of the lights). The Fargo Forum also maintained this belief, proclaiming that "Balfour was easily the brightest, cleanest little city west of the Twin Cities."

Alas the promise faded and like so much of North Dakota, Balfour became an exporter -- an exporter of people. This occured to such an extent that by 1990 there are but 33 bona fide residents that call Balfour home. Nevertheless, if you are travelling along U.S. 52 and happen to come to Latitude 47 48' 30" Longitude 100 30', do stop at the cafe along the highway. The booths may be cramped, but the food is better than good and the conversation is reliably honest Americana.

An 1894 passenger train at Balfour. Note the twelve foot wide portable depot which was part of the construction train. This was replaced in 1901 by moving the Kenmare depot in sections down the main line. Below one sees the depot being consumed by fire in 1908.

Lyle Weidler Collection

"On March 22, 1908, the Soo depot burst into flames, Agent Owen, his wife and her sister barely having time to escape from the upper window. After Owen had succeeded in getting Mrs. Owen and Julia out, he fell at the window with exhaustion. He credits Dr. Stone for pulling him out and saving his life. Flames leaped out and scorched Doc's moustache, hair and eyebrows. The building burned quickly and practially all the contents were lost. A big crowd gathered but little could be done but to squirt chemicals on the sidewalks, pull box cars out of danger and save Shorty Overholzer's wagons. The roof of Dr. Stone's house caught fire but prompt action saved it. Jack, the best known dog in town, with piteous farewell cry, lay down to be consumed in the flames. Poor Jack, only a dog but everybody in town felt sorry."
BALFOUR MESSENGER, MARCH 26, 1908.

The new Balfour depot in 1909. This building has now been moved to Drake for historical display.

Pete Bonesteel Collection

Richard Yaremko

The blue skies of North Dakota—vast, yet intimate. Above **6609** and **775** (both SD-40-2's) drift by a small pond near Kenmare on May 26, 1993.

Right: Norma's pristine depot (Fall 1953).

Below right: Soo/BN (former Great Northern) crossing tower at Minot.

Below: a wide curve in the wide open space near Portal—July, 1991.

J. David Ingles

Byron Knutson

Gerald Olson

Balfour baseball team travelling via Soo to baseball tournament at Velva June 6, 1907. Although it is but 28 miles to Velva, roads were very primitive and horse and wagon travel was extremely time consuming. Music organizations, sports and the ever popular Chautauqua all travelled by train even for what seems to us rather short distances during the early part of the twentieth century.

Lyle Weidler

"HOGBACK RIDGE" air view to the northwest of Balfour. U.S. Highway 52 and the Soo mainline run together and appear to cross what seems an old railroad grade. Not so - the whitish line running from the bottom left towards the top right is a drumlin. It is the longest and most famous in North Dakota. Nearly straight for 16 miles, it is nearly 300 feet in width and at times up to 50 feet high. Drumlins and similar topographic features are referred to as glacial ice thrust masses. Other (non drumlin) ice thrust masses seen from Soo tracks include "Hawks Nest" near Carrington as well as the "Alkabo Moraine" in Divide County near Alkabo.

John. P. Bluemle

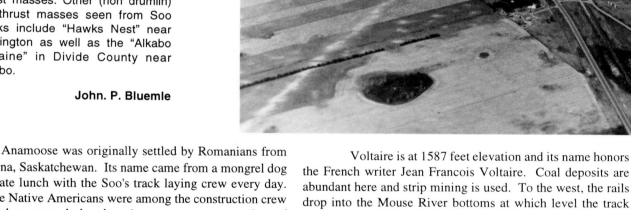

Anamoose was originally settled by Romanians from Regina, Saskatchewan. Its name came from a mongrel dog that ate lunch with the Soo's track laying crew every day. Some Native Americans were among the construction crew and they named the dog Anamoose—a corruption of Chippewa for 'hungry dog.' Although initially prosperous with a population of 669 in 1910, there were but 222 residents in 1990.

Flax had been the dominant crop here about the turn of the century, but today wheat, and sunflowers reign—the Cargill elevator markets 3,000,000 bushels of grain each year.

East of Anamoose are high moraines on both sides of the line, whereas if one looks west from Anamoose, one sees a large valley with terraces on the sides whose flat bottom lacks a stream—a remnant of an old glacial river.

Drake, seven miles west, is the junction for lines to Fordville as well as west to Sanish (New Town) and Bismarck. Continuing our journey west, we cross the Wintering River before reaching Balfour.

Voltaire is at 1587 feet elevation and its name honors the French writer Jean Francois Voltaire. Coal deposits are abundant here and strip mining is used. To the west, the rails drop into the Mouse River bottoms at which level the track continues into Minot. Velva (some 459 miles west and north of Minneapolis) is the start of rather spectacular coulee country. U.S. Highway 52 continues to follow the line through this beautiful valley on to Minot.

Minot (1990 population 34,544) is another city where the Soo had to play second fiddle by getting there last. The Great Northern arrived and made this a division point which not only was true in 1890, but also in the 1990's as headquarters for Burlington Northern's Dakota Division. A large Air Force base complex, Minot State University, the North Dakota State Fair and October's Host Fest all bring support and tourists to this, the fourth largest city, in the Flickertail State.

J. David Ingles

The Minot freighthouse was used as the agent's office after passenger service was discontinued and the most unique passenger depot was closed. Until the early 1990s yard clerks had their offices in this building. Until 1993 the signal maintainers, linemen and section crews were also headquartered here. (They are now at the enginehouse in Minot).

Built in 1908 it is 50' X 211' with two stories as shown in the office part. The freight storage room had 14' studs and was used until the late sixties when L.C.L. service was discontinued.

Mouse River was the original settlement name of this McHenry County village. As the Soo continued west in 1893, it was renamed Velva. Much lignite coal underlies this area with mines and power production nearby. The surface supports cattle ranching with the bottom lands of the Mouse River valley being a good source of hay.

1952 Postcard View, Pete Bonesteel Collection

Below: Velva's Second Class Soo Standard depot with a Fairmont speeder on patrol during the summer of 1970. Eric Severaid of television fame was born here in 1912.

Burlington, some eight miles northwest of Minot, has today become a suburb of that city. It was originally prosperous after having been reached by Soo rails in 1893; the nearby lignite fields and even a brick factory shipped via the Soo. Although it had been the original county seat of Ward County, Burlington lost the courthouse to Minot in 1888. Here one finds the confluence of the Mouse and Des Lacs rivers. The line lies in the Des Lacs valley for some forty miles. The Des Lacs is a remarkable small stream characterized by scant fall. After Donnybrook in fact, the river flares out into a series of shallow long narrow lakes.

John Gjevre

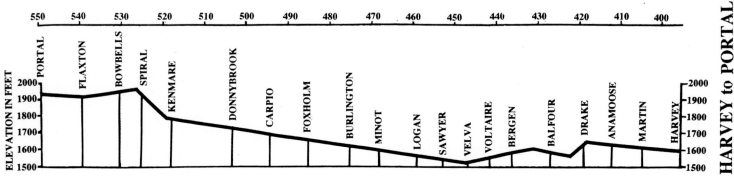

HARVEY to PORTAL

Spiral, N.D. It was quite a sight in 1916 to see grain threshed in a field where a hastily built siding from the Soo allowed the farmer to bring box cars down to his threshing machine. This saved miles of haulage at that time since there were no elevators at Spiral. The rough track reminds one of logging railroads and I would suspect that the steam engine for the threshing was used to move cars back and forth to the main line.

***In the Des Lacs Valley**—train No. 570:* Bohi first encountered this train at Roche Percee, a hamlet just south of Estevan, Saskatchewan. During an hour long stop at Portal, customs work was done while **4433** was added. The Des Lacs Valley is one of the longest scenic stretches along the Soo main line in North Dakota. 12:05 July 17, 1992

Charles Bohi

K E N M A R E

Soo Line survey crew having dinner in 1905.

Perhaps the names are long forgotten, but the Wheat Line remains in 1994, a monument in tie and rail to a survey well done.

Paul Carlson Collection

E. H. Gross Photo

Above and to the left are views of track laying on the completed Wheat Line grade near Kenmare in 1905.

Paul Carlson Collection
Both photos by E.H. Gross

Below- Kenmare 1906 - The Wheat Line construction train is tied up. Note the bunk cars which are later to become portable depots and other trackside structures.

Paul Carlson Collection

September 1905 - View of Kenmare taken from the Soo Line water tower showing roundhouse and turntable under construction. Des Lac's Lake is in the right background.

Lawrence Drabus Photo

Lawrence Drabus

Same turntable 1943.

A 1943 view of the roundhouse—originally built with four stalls, then enlarged to six stalls when the Flaxton line was extended to Montana, and thereafter cut back to three stalls in the 1930's. (Note the frogs because of the steep angle to the turntable).

To the right is again the same turntable June 1988. The only use is for occasional engine turning power for the Wheat and Whitetail Lines.

Photo by Otto Dobnick

To the right: Kenmare depot and freight house about 1907. That's an H-1 Pacific on the point of the 3 car passenger train. To the right is a flat car, loaded with a steam engine for farm use.

E.H. Gross Photo. Paul Carlson Collection

Kenmare is surrounded by fields of lignite coal, a soft coal found abundantly in west central North Dakota. Below is a view of the electric generation plant. Note: stock cars are pressed into coal hauling.

Another view of Kenmare, showing the tool shed and the section foreman's house with the downtown in the background (about 1907).

E.H. Gross Photo. Paul Carlson Collection

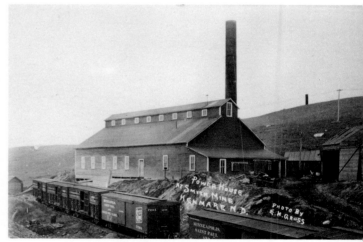

"Steamer" Gordon Fawcett and Barge Taking Grain at Newport for Kenmare, N.D.

To the left is a view of the lake steamboat "Gordon Fawcett" and barge taking on wheat and flax at Newport on Des Lac's Lake for shipment to Kenmare and subsequent transfer to Soo boxcars for the journey east. Around the turn of the century, the Soo Line published joint water and rail tariffs for grain movements from Newport to Minneapolis.

E.H. Gross Photo. Paul Carlson Collection

Five hundred and twenty miles northwest of Shoreham at 1799 feet of elevation lies Kenmare in the valley of the Des Lacs. The railroad is built very nearly at lake (river) level. The town proper is built on a beautiful hill and the main business district is built around a town square park which has been enriched following the relocation of a Danish-style windmill which for many years was used by an area farmer to grind grain for flour and feed. Should one travel through Kenmare, the author certainly recommends a stop at the 'White Buffalo Soda Fountain,' a truly authentic, functioning, turn of the century relic in the Carlson Drug Store.

Kenmare was platted in 1899 and named from Kenmare, Ireland. Kenmare got its initial boost when a Thomas ward who was Soo section foreman at Spiral to the north opened a livery barn here in 1896. At that time the settlement was called Lignite on account of the abundant coal that appeared in seams along the nearby coulees. His livery service had a special wagon to accommodate new settlers on survey trips to look for a homestead site. In 1897, the Soo built special immigrant sheds–20 feet by 100 feet long–with ten small rooms. Here, in these cramped quarters, incoming pioneer families lived while they reconnoitered their homesteads. This thoughtfulness of the Soo's immigration department allowed some comfort compared to the earlier settlers as they settled end erected places on their homesteads.

By 1903, enterprising residents set up grain buying stations at various points along the Upper Des Lacs Lake. One A. A. Robinson of Minot had elevators at Patterson, Newport and Pleasant on the lake. It is reported that Robinson shipped 200,000 bushels of grain by lake barge the following year. A photograph of barge traffic at Newport appears on these pages from around this period.

Right: SD 40-2 **757** and GP-9 **2410** leave the Portal yard with tonnage in tow. It is common to have bulkhead flats carrying lumber east at all times of the year on the mainline.

Dennis Schmidt

The name E. H. Gross is synomonous with early photographic history of the 'gooseneck portion' of Ward County and surrounding Burke and Renville Counties. Gross was a pioneer optometrist and jeweler arriving in 1902. His enthusiastic passion with glass plate photography captured virtually all aspects of area life including the magnificient views reproduced on these pages by the courtesy of Paul Carlson. He continued to work as a jeweler until his death at the age of 91 in 1971.

Portal

Portal is aptly named, for it is here that settlers and traffic moved–through to the prairie provinces of Saskatchewan and Alberta as well as to the Pacific Northwest during the early years of this century. At that time the **Soo-Spokane Train Deluxe** went through here to the Canadian Pacific main and over to Medicine Hat. From there it went over the Crow's Nest line of the Canadian Pacific to Spokane and down the Spokane International to Portland.

Portal was reached by Soo rails August 25, 1893 as the line was extended that year from Cathay (about 100 miles southeast of Minot). For a detailed description of Soo Line construction methods used 100 years ago, please refer to pp 22-24 *Part I*.

Initially, Soo crews operated on CP rails as far as Estevan, but as traffic increased the CP built their own yards and thus both Portal and North Portal became terminal towns.

PORTAL, USA | NORTH PORTAL, CANADA

Stuart Nelson Collection

Left to right: Depot, Customs, and Immigration Buildings.

George Stancel Collection

The diagonal white line is the international boundary and the Grand Hotel stands to the right. The proximity of the Soo's depot to this line is very evident. (About 1937)

Tom Reiersgard Collection
1911 view of the Grand Hotel.

Today freight only stops for the mandatory customs clearance, the engines and train will run through–sometimes from Chicago to Vancouver. Yet, Portal remains the portal, the gateway to the Canadian prairies and beyond. The Harvey crew will lay over and return to Harvey with another manifest. Portal, however small, is a most needed outpost at the far end of the Soo.

Below: the bareness of the prairie contrasts with the busy CP freight yards in North Portal, 1913.

Crosby Museum and Historical Society

Floyd Swenson Jr.

1961: The Canadian Pacific was still using a few steam engines and they put one on the very eastbound Dominion to North Portal. That's Ollie Walden, a Soo conductor, walking towards the train. Soon a Soo FP 7 will be attached for the final trip to Minneapolis.

92

Above:and Below: Birdseye views of North Portal, Saskatchewan, Canada (circa 1908).

Crosby Museum and Historical Society

Mary Sjue Collection

Above: Portal's engine house with turntable behind and ice house in the left background. Incidentally, this engine house was moved from Pollock, S.D.

Right: Ominous clouds during a March day (1992) threaten the no longer used Portal ice house while wheel sets await transport back to Shoreham for rehabilitation.

Mary Sjue Collection

Soo Pump house at Portal.   **Mary Sjue Collection**

Mary Sjue Collection

Portal Water tower, 1949. Someone forgot to shut the pump off yielding this amusing result.

Troops off to WWII in 1942.   **Mary Sjue Collection**

Cat Patrol! The overfed mouser works her floor in the ever busy Portal depot in 1991. Since then the CP/Soo has built an entirely new depot. 'Wonder if they still need the cat?

Mary Sjue Collection

734 balances on Portal's turntable. This was one of only four GP 40's owned by the Soo prior to the Milwaukee Road acquisition in 1985. This unit was renumbered **4602.**

Larry Easton

Terminal Development In Portal

1893	Depot 24' x 92' was built, two stories the entire length.
1898	4 Stall round house. Joint Soo/CP bunk house.
1904	Restaurant and Hotel, Custom house with two stories. Car repair shop.
1905	Additional stalls added to roundhouse. Custom house addition, 20' x 24', and Immigration building 28' x 32', two stories
1931	Roundhouse: four stalls destroyed by fire.
1935	Old two story depot razed.
1942	Custom house remodeled into depot, with removal of second floor. Second floor also removed from immigration building.
1953	1911 ice house razed, new ice house built.
1955	End of steam service, coal shed and water tower torn down.
1967	Roundhouse was torn down; Pollock, SD enginehouse moved to Portal.
1993	New depot, old depot removed.

Mary Sjue Collection

M M Circular No. 18
Minneapolis - September 28, 1945

To All Section Foremen,
  B&B Foremen,
  Roadmasters,

This summer we had a fire in one of the stockyards which caused $1,650 damage. In attempting to determine the cause of the fire it develops that several boys had been in the stockyards immediately preceding the discovery of the fire. The boys all denied that they had in any way been responsible for same and the parents of one claimed that a train passed the yard just shortly before the fire was discovered and that probably it was caused by a spark from the engine.

If at any time you see anybody, whether transients or boys, in the yards not in connection with handling shipments of stock you will immediately see that they leave the premises, warning them that if necessary the local authorities will be called upon the police the premises.

Please acknowledge,
  T.Z. Krumm

cc/ All Engineers

Quarantine yard at North Portal 1913. Quarantine was necessary to diminish diseases crossing the border. The Canadian government stationed a veterinarian at this site. Likewise, the United States had a cattle immigrant shed at Kenmare for the same purpose.

Tom Reiersgard Collection

STOCKYARDS

In 1912 the Drake Stockyard appears to be a newly constructed 64' by 64' standard two penyard.

Gordon Twedt Collection

Stock trains and stockyards were a necessary complement to the grain elevator and boxcars for almost all western railroads up to relatively recent times. Smaller meat packing plants, feed lots and changes in marketing have dramatically changed the pattern of the meat industry across the west. There are two major reasons for the demise of the cattle train, the first being the ability of a semi–trailer stock truck to pick up loads at individual farmers' and feed lots . Secondly, agribusiness firms not only own feed lots, but in addition they have fleets of trucks which haul cattle to and from the feed lots. Because of this vertical integration these same tractor units carry the necessary feed from other farms or elevators to their own lots. It is true that some large feed lots have private railroad hopper car fleets for haulage of feed grains by rail, but such operations are rare.

Larry Easton, Photo

A rather typical cattle car — very 'plain Jane' and utilitarian. The Soo owned no 'modern' all steel cars. In the off-season these cars could be seen hauling ties in railroad service.

Up until World War II, most western Minnesota, North and South Dakota and Montana communities had railroad stockyards. The Soo Line had a standard design and the majority of yards were a two pen 64' x 64' and each yard would have a well, feed rack and a six ton capacity Victor stock scale. Other common sizes were a 3 pen 64' x 96' and a 4 pen 64' x 128'. Small sites not needing a pen would be provided with a chute at the siding for direct loading from truck to cattle car.

The Enderlin yard started as a 9 pen yard in 1893 and had expanded to 96 pens by 1923. It was one of the very largest yards and its pens would serve as holding areas for the satisfaction of the 48 hour rule. (The 48 hour rule is described later in this chapter). During peak years 150 carloads of livestock could be fed and watered in Enderlin before going on to South St. Paul for slaughter.

The magnitude of stock shipments can be understood by the cattle drives of the N-N Cattle Company and others. Cattle were herded and driven from as far as northeastern Montana across the prairie to

Below: men are herding a Hereford up the cattle chute. As a young boy, the author and friends would play by walking on fence tops of the then no longer used Soo stockyard in Rosholt.

Don Mahoney

Crosby Museum and Historical Society

In extreme Northwestern North Dakota, Ambrose had a rather large yard, especially when compared to the Drake yard on the preceding page. The three largest yards, however, were at Portal, Enderlin, and Shoreham.

Spiral, a siding north of present day Kenmare. The Soo simply did not have stockpens for cattle drives of this magnitude as reportedly 125,000 cattle were shipped in 1894 alone. Hence, the ranchers of necessity built acres of corrals from native poles. If one realizes that a cattle car in those days held about 25 head, then it seems mind boggling that the new road could and did handle this movement in a single year.

The federal 48 hour rule specified that cattle, pigs and sheep were only allowed to be on board a cattle car for up to 48 hours. After that time it was mandatory for humane reasons that the animals be removed from a car, be fed and watered. The adoption of the 48 hour rule implied that trains carrying stock would have priority just below that of passenger trains. In order to have only one such priority train a week on each line it became necessary to have stock pickup days. Thus it became that on the Drake and Wheat lines Saturday was stock train day and on the Winnipeg division the stock cars traveled on Tuesdays. The forty eight hour rule was eventually revised to 24 hrs and only 36 hours with an extension signed by the shipper.

Each shipper would contact the depot agent prior to stock day so that there would be an ample supply of stock cars spotted at the yards where necessary. Shippers were allowed to bring livestock to the yard up to 48 hours before shipping time. Actual loading of the stockcars did not occur until shortly before the train arrived. Sometimes loading would still be in progress at

Stockyards at Fullerton, North Dakota circa 1925.

Eugene Simak Collection

the time the crew arrived and the engine would spot the cars as the loading continued.

Even during the decade following World War II, much cattle moved over Soo rails. For example, Sanish, ND shipped 382 cars of livestock in 1947.

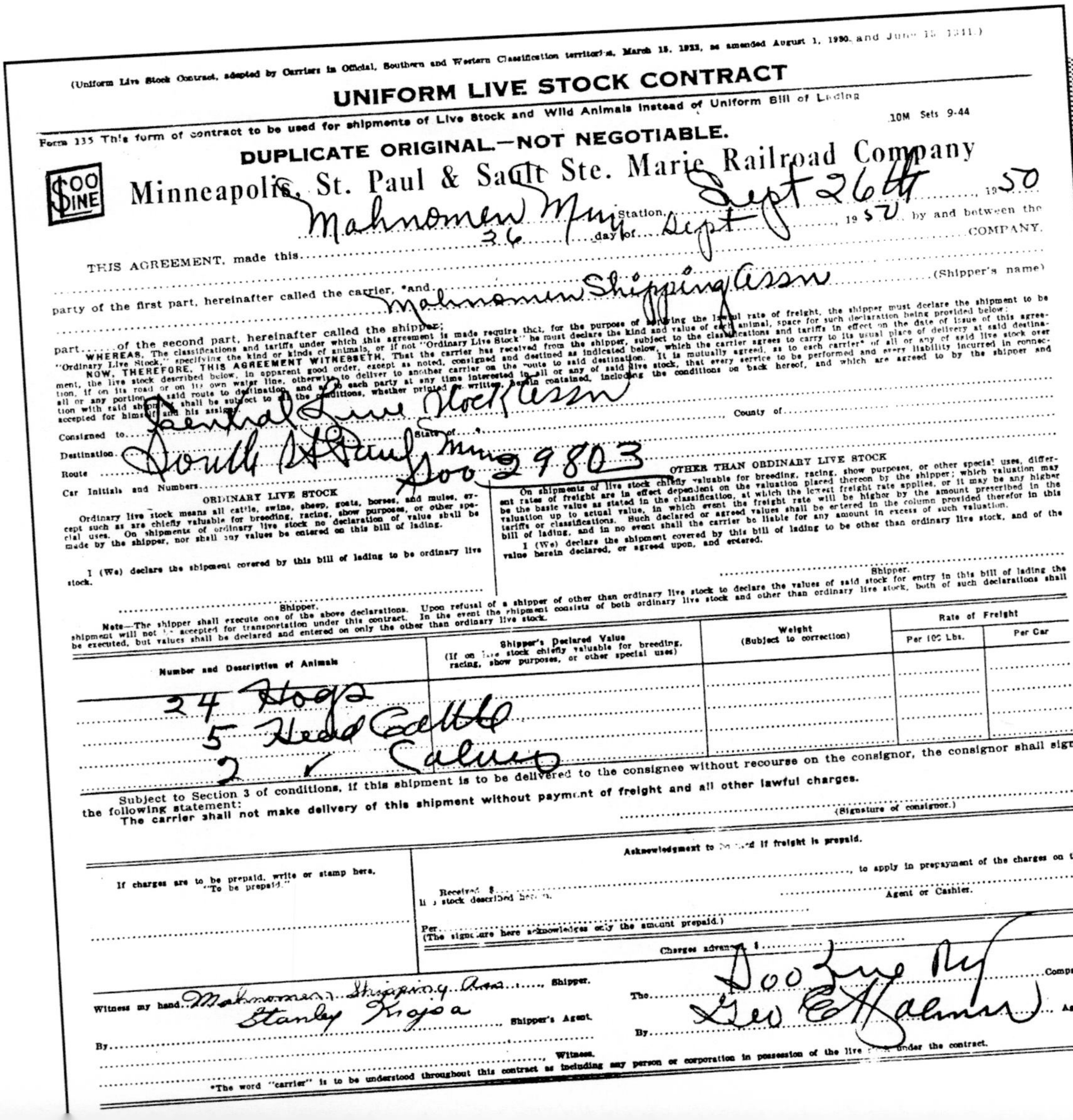

(Uniform Live Stock Contract, adopted by Carriers in Official, Southern and Western Classification territories, March 15, 1922, as amended August 1, 1930, and June 15, 1941.)

UNIFORM LIVE STOCK CONTRACT

To be used for shipments of Live Stock and Wild Animals instead of Uniform Bill of Lading

Form 135 This form of contract to be used for shipments of Live Stock and Wild Animals.

10M Sets 9-44

DUPLICATE ORIGINAL.—NOT NEGOTIABLE.

Minneapolis, St. Paul & Sault Ste. Marie Railroad Company

Mahnomen, Minn Station,

THIS AGREEMENT, made this......36......day of....Sept.....19 50....by and between the......................COMPANY.

party of the first part, hereinafter called the carrier, *and... Mahnomen Shipping Assn (Shipper's name)

[body of contract with handwritten entries]

Consigned to... Central Live Stock Assn

Destination... South St Paul Minn

County of...

Route... Soo 9803

Car Initials and Numbers...

Number and Description of Animals	Shipper's Declared Value	Weight (Subject to correction)	Rate of Freight Per 100 Lbs.	Per Car
34 Hogs				
5 Head Cattle				
2 Calves				

Witness my hand... Mahnomen Shipping Assn ... Shipper.
Stanley Krajsa ... Shipper's Agent.

The... Soo Line Ry ...Company.
Geo C Palmer ...Agent.

In order to capture the flavor of cattle movements at the turn of the century it is fun and instructive to read this reconstructed letter of Swedish immigrant Marten writing his relative back in the old land.

St.Paul, Minnesota
Friday- Nov. 15, 1912

Dear Bengta,

I am writing to you as I wait in the stockyards at St. Paul for our return train. I am in the midst of my annual cattle selling trip - this year a carload of yearling steers and another of sheep.

We loaded on the Soo Line at Comstock, went to Drake, then southeast to Hankinson where we switched to Great Northern tracks. Because of Ola's continuing interest, I have sketched a map of our route.

Cattle prices are only fair this year, but we've had a wet season for good pasture so the steers and lambs were heavier than usual. The sales check was for more than I had estimated, so I'll be able to pay off both the John Hancock mortgage as well as a note at the First National Bank in Brinsmade. I had to borrow money last fall from Beisbarth - he's the president of the bank - to get through threshing. The hired men deserve their pay on time.

Oscar - he's 13 now - and three of the hired men are along on this trip. I bring some of the men along each year to help unload and load the cattle when we stop for feed and water. When we ship cattle the Soo lets us ride free in the caboose. The men also get to spend a night in St. Paul. I never have a problem finding volunteers to help ship cattle. Oscar's eyes get wide at the sights and he is, I'm sure, secretly enjoying missing a few days of school. - - -

- - - On the trip down it was nightfall as we rolled through Fessenden and Carrington towards Valley City. From our perch in the caboose, we could see stacks (of straw) burning brightly in the distance. Oscar said they looked to him like golden stars that had fallen to earth.

Our return train should leave early tomorrow morning. I hope the hired men make it back from Snoose Boulevard in time.

Wasn't that something about the Titanic? Ella and I both remember how cold that North Atlantic was. - - -

I think I'll walk over to the cafe to see if I can buy a plug of CLIMAX to chew.

With affection,

Marten

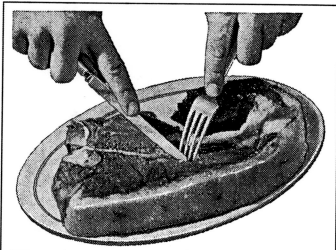

Note: It is of interest that the Drake line had only opened during 1912 and the map also shows the old cattle drive route. Snoose Boulevard referred to the 'Seven Corners' area along Cedar Avenue in Minneapolis, a favorite meeting and 'watering' place for Scandinavian immigrants the early years of this century. It was standard practice for the Soo and other railroads that the shipper and one or two of his crew to receive round trip ticket to accompany the stock. They traveled in the caboose to market and as tourist class in a passenger car on return.

We are indebted to Richard Hofstrand, Ph.D. for permission to reprint the above passage from his book *With Affection, Marten* copyright 1983.

The Whitetail Sub
the Western Reach of the Soo

Flaxton in 1893 was but a well, a water tank, and a section house. In 1899, a sidetrack was laid and in 1901, the town was platted and named Flaxton because flax was a major crop which grew well due to the cool summer nights.

The Seibert Hotel was built in Flaxton in 1909, becoming one of the finest hotels in northwestern N.D. President William Howard Taft once stayed here, and the Duke and Duchess of Windsor visited it in 1948.

Today's declining population of 121 mirrors the ongoing urbanization of North Dakota, as well as that of the United States as a whole. Oil in the area is an important 'cash crop' for those people fortunate enough to own the mineral rights. In 1905, the Soo graded west to Ambrose making Flaxton a junction town with a yard, a one stall engine house, and a turning wye.

Crosby, county seat of Divide County, dates from 1903 when the Great Northern made its terminal here. The Soo came in 1905 and originally platted Imperial three miles east of Crosby. The town lasted but two years before the Great Northern and Soo passed the peace pipe. In 1907, the Soo would give up Imperial in exchange for the Great Northern abandoning McCumber for the Soo's Rolette along the Wheat Line.

It remained until 1913 for the Soo to look westward again with the grading and rail-laying from Ambrose out to Whitetail through the North Dakota communities of Colgan, Fortuna, and Alkabo, paralleling the Canadian border line. The Sheridan County communities of Raymond, Outlook, Daleview (formerly Ranous) and Whitetail were all established in Montana during the same year. Each of these ranching (and now oil) towns have had their own individual triumphs and failures. Of local lore, the story of Hominy Thompson deserves special mention.

Oil wells can be seen along much of the Whitetail Sub all the way into Sheridan County in Montana. Originally, the line went through Columbus, Kermit, and Crosby, but after World War II, long-time rivals Great Northern and Soo entered into an agreement whereby the

Crosby Historical Museum

Imperial North Dakota - 1907 view. This was a community which the Soo gave up on. Crosby became the county seat, and the entire town was moved to Crosby three miles distant. The town was under construction, however, in this 1907 view.

TWIN CITIES - WHITETAIL, MONT.					
Read Down					**Read Up**
	3 51 Ex. Sat.	Miles	**TABLE 34**	4 52 Ex. Mo	
	P. M.			A. M.	
	9 35	0.0	Lv St. Paul (C.T.)...Ar	7 15	
	⑧10 25	10.9	Lv Minneapolis.....Ar	Ⓔ6 30	
	1 50	552.0	Ar Flaxton.........Lv	3 44	
	† 2 00	552.0	Lv Flaxton (10)....Ar	† 1 00	
	f 2 20	561.9	* Rival............Lv	f12 40	Round
	2 45	569.7	* Columbus........ *	12 20	Trip
	3 15	581.7	* Kermit.......... *	11 50	Tickets
	3 50	593.1	* Crosby.......... *	11 20	Save You
	4 35	602.4	* Ambrose......... *	10 25	Time and
	4 35	608.8	* Colgan.......... *	10 10	Money
	5 00	616.5	* Fortuna......... *	9 50	
	5 25	623.0	* Alkabo.......... *	9 20	
	6 00	631.8	* Westby, Mont.... *	9 00	
	6 15	635.6	* McElroy......... *	8 45	
	6 30	641.7	* Comertown....... *	8 25	
	6 50	649.7	* Dooley.......... *	8 05	
	7 10	658.4	* ⑧ Raymond....... *	7 45	
	7 40	667.9	* Outlook......... *	7 20	
	f 8 00	675.9	* Daleview........ *	f 7 00	
	8 30	688.0	Ar Whitetail......Lv	6 30	
	P. M.			A. M.	

TIMETABLE FROM 1947 SCHEDULE

Below: Crosby, 1907. This town became county seat of Divide County with two railroads (GN and Soo). It remains a ranching center and boasts an award-winning newspaper, and a successfully complete county musuem and historical society.

Crosby Museum and Historical Society

Un bel di —one fine day in June 1976 has been immortalized in Kodachrome by A. J. Sutherland. Daleview, above and at right, with F7's **2201B** and **501C**. Below is the same consist at Outlook on the Whitetail line.

A. J. Sutherland

A. J. Sutherland

Below: The prairie is the Soo's flower garden. Thundering red, white and black horses conquer the West.

Soo Line Railroad

Below: west of Raymond, MT in lonesome Sheridan County **4405,** a GP38-2, was a well-seasoned eleven year old this 29th of June, 1988.

Otto Dobnick

Outlook, Montana August 1930. The town is now 17 years old and still bears all the appearance of the Western frontier. The town's hotel is just above the 'Look out for the cars' sign. Two girls are playing tennis on this side of the Outlook Cafe, and the Texaco gas pump is waiting for customers (2nd building in on the right). Trees are slow to grow here, and the drought will continue for many more years. At this time, Sam Thompson was depot agent.

The One Man Siege of 'Hominy' Thompson

Sheridan County, Montana was in the national news during 1923 as Elmer E. 'Hominy' Thompson single-handedly defied the Soo Line for 13 days by blocking tracks and railroad right-of-way near Daleview on the Whitetail line.

The Soo had built this line into Montana some ten years earlier and Hominy was upset over the meagerness of the $2400 that the railroad had offered him for disrupting his irrigation ditches. Hominy, (who was the first white settler in Sheridan County) was among the last of the colorful plainsmen. He had built a dugout cabin along the banks of Whitetail creek in 1894. This humble shack remained his home until 1929 except for those fateful 13 days in 1923.

The siege was to start after he had countless disappointments in his negotiations with Soo officials in his attempts to get what he felt was a fair compensation for the railroad's disruption. Hominy built a tar paper shack on the railroad's right-of-way and tore up some rails. He used his wits, plus a six shooter and a Winchester rifle to keep the Soo at bay. Finally, in exasperation the railroad called the Federal Marshal in to arrest Hominy on charges of obstructing delivery of the U.S. Mail.

Needless to say - Hominy lost that war but was never defeated. He died December 23, 1949 in Plentywood at the age of 87. He was well read to the end and folks who had visited him during his days along the banks of Whitetail creek remarked that the dirt floor of his dugout shanty was always swept and that his clothes were freshly washed. He truly was one of the last of the tenacious frontiersmen of the old west.

The Daleview Lumber Yard Building moving west to Whitetail via the Soo. This was one of the first buildings to be moved out of Daleview as the depression strengthened its grip on rural America.

The railroad depot at Ranous, pictured here with one of the earliest pioneers, Lon Desonia, on the white horse. Due to similar town names within the state along the Soo Line to the east, the pioneers got together, at the request of the U.S. Postal Department, and renamed Ranous as Daleview.

102

Otto Dobnick

Sheridan County in Montana, and Divide County in N.D. are the two most oil-rich areas served by the Soo. East of Outlook, Montana. (6-29-88)

John Tysse Jr. Collection

Triple-headed snowplow expedition enters a cut four miles east of Raymond. (February 1916)

Below: The last steam-powered passenger train to Whitetail Montana. Exactly 676.4 miles west of Shoreham, and a mere seven miles south of the Canadian border. Mixed train service, however, did continue with diesel power for several more years.

Lawrence Draybus

103

Unit train activity at Whitetail

August 1988 - these three views of a unit train at the end of the Soo in Sheridan County, Montana show the size (52 cars) and the challenges smaller elevators across the west had to meet and solve in order to receive the lower tariffs of bulk unit trains. As is seen in the middle photo, the elevator employee was attempting to bridge the grain spout across the car on the track nearest the elevator when the not unexpected happened.

Bottom photo: looking west, an International Car Company extended vision caboose brings up the rear of the train as the cars are to be spotted for loading. Whitetail was as far west as Soo tracks could go. Today, the line from Flaxton to Whitetail is leased to the Dakota, Missouri Valley and Western and this shortline operates out of Kenmare with trackage rights on the Soo mainline.

All Photographs by Cory Tryan

A New Line is Born 1913...

Above Left: Deep into a cut the grading progresses the Soo Line into Montana.

Bodine Photo, Sam Bloom Collection

Above: Rear view of the tractor-pulled elevating grader, a 'mucker,' grading the new line near Alkabo.

1913 Photo by Bodine, Sam Bloom Collection

Left: A construction train enters Alkabo in 1913 with a D-2 mogul.

Miller Lake, southwest of Alkabo, has a large deposit of Glauber's salt (sodium sulfate) estimated at about 5,000,000 ton. Following World War II a plant was built at the dry lake site to exploit the salt commercially, but shipments on the Soo were few and the opportunity still exists for future development.

...and the line will haul grain

1984

A pair of GP-38-2's, 4432 and 4441 at Ambrose, ND with westbound Kenmare-Whitetail local freight. The entire train consist was empties destined for grain loading on the Whitetail branch. Noon: May 21, 1984.

Bob Wise

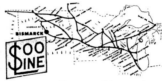
A 'caboose hop' rests along the old Missouri valley division
(circa 1910).

State Historical Society of North Dakota

Bismarck, 1969   **Soo Line Railroad**

Bismarck was founded in 1872/73 and named
for the Chancellor of Germany at that time in order to
please German investors in the Northern Pacific Railroad
which reached there in 1872. It became the state capital
of North Dakota in 1889 and Soo Line tracks reached it
in 1902.

The six stall, brick, veneer roundhouse was
built in 1906 and 1908, but a 61' turntable was installed
in 1903. The 20' x 120' freight depot was built in 1902
and enlarged in 1906, and the 24' x 73' passenger depot
(a stub end terminal type) was built in 1902 and retired
in 1968 when the new 24' x 40' hip-roofed office
building (see page 110 in *Saga of the Soo Part I*) was put
into use.

The Soo line yards and roundhouse area are
now parking lots for the medical center/hospital
complex— and Dakota and Missouri Valley
locomotives use Soo tracks and trackage-rights under
lease from Oakes to Washburn.

Missouri River Country

The story of the Bismarck, Washburn and Great Falls Railway is detailed in *Part I* pp. 112-119. The following is a description of not only that line (Bismarck to Washburn and on to Coleharbor) which the Soo Line purchased in 1904, but also of the line through Max and on to Drake on the main line.

Burleigh and McLean counties in North Dakota still had Northern Pacific Land Grant lands unsold in 1899. Some 113,000 acres of these lands were bought by W.D. Washburn at $1.00 per acre and advertised to settlers at $6.50 to $8.50 an acre with the new rail line's presence. This Washburn was the first president of both the Minneapolis and Pacific as well as the Minneapolis, Sault St. Marie Railways.

The first station north from Bismarck Washburn named for his son-in-law Frank Baldwin. The author's brother was relief depot agent at Baldwin in 1949 and a photo of the depot as it then appeared is found on page 102 of *Part I*. This 16' x 34' frame depot was retired in 1968.

The Wilton depot, although of frame construction and only 20' x 90' would arguably become one of the most interesting architectural monuments of the Soo (details are discussed in *Part I*). Today, the depot has been moved off the right-of-way and is part of a town museum containing an elaborate HO model railroad in its old freight room.

Wilton, like Baldwin, also had a 24' x 16' wood tub water tower and a 20' Eclipse windmill. A coaling station with its derrick house, twelve buckets and one lorry, and a standard coaling ramp were used in the days of steam.

Wilton depot as originally constructed about 1904. Note the Bismarck, Washburn and Great Falls passenger coach to the left of depot structures.

State Historical Society of North Dakota

Above: 1904 Postcard view of the Washburn Lignite Mine.

Douglas Wick Collection

Wilton, W.D. Washburn's 'own' town, home of his coal mines and the distinctive Pagoda Depot. By 1912, Wilton was a thriving mining and ranching community. Both the Soo and Northern Pacific provided service, and from the photo it would seem that the area folk had time and money to travel.

Gary Anderson Collection

Soo Standard 4-4-0 **27** with the frame for its homemade wooden sweep plow at the coal dock siding Bismarck about 1912. Not only is the frame worn and battered, but just look at the mangled headlight!

State Historical Society

No. 257 Bismarck-Drake passenger local at Max circa 1920. Henry A. Windmueller, Brakeman; Roscoe Goddard, Engineer. This train convieniently connected at Drake with No. 105 to provide a rather lengthy (seven hours) ride to Minot.

Stuart Nelson Collection

This country is most suited for cattle grazing, but, in addition, for almost 90 years coal mines have provided substantial employment (see pages 117, 118 of *Part I*).

North from Wilton there was a passenger stop known as "Merida." According to Douglas Wick, Joseph 'Billy' Jennings led a group of neighbors in privately building a grain and cattle shipping facility here.

At Washburn (45 miles north from Bismarck), an elaborate layout was necessitated by the transfer elevator to the Benton Packet Company (see *Part I*). This was a gas-powered boat line on the Missouri River that served upstream well into Montana. It would bring wheat and other grain downstream for transshipment on the Soo to eastern markets. It also took coal (from the nearby Wilton mines) as well as settlers's goods and

commodities upstream as far as and onto the Yellowstone River in Montana. Washburn also had a water tank and stockyards. It is also worth noting, that Washburn was named after Cadwallader Colden Washburn (1818-1882), a brother of William D. Washburn. This community (population 1506) has boomed today because of the nearby coal mines and electric generation facilities. Washburn was founded in 1882 by 'King John' Satterlund, a Swedish promoter who had moved into the area earlier. He and a John S. Veeder started a store which became the stage stop north of Bismarck. It quickly became an important river boat stop for steamboat traffic from St. Louis to Montana. By 1901, when the Bismarck, Washburn and Great Falls Railway had reached Washburn, steamboat traffic had dwindled and thereafter the packet boats of Isaac Baker's Benton Packet line plied the Missouri. The last sternwheeler on

Above: 1937 view of the Underwood depot.

Daryl Thompson photo

Below: 1912 post card view of the Underwood depot, water tank and windmill. At that time, this little Missouri River village boasted five elevators in addition to a flour mill.

Gordon Twedt Collection

Elevators-Flour Mill Underwood N.D.

1953: **369**, an Alco RSC-2 1500 horsepower is slowly drifting through Coleharbor. Both Alco road switchers as well as the Baldwin 1500 horsepower road switchers were extensively used on all the branch lines in North Dakota.

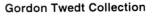

The first station west of Drake on the Missouri River Line is Kief, an alternate spelling of Kiev, Ukraine from whence many of the early settlers originated.

Below: On a New Town job, **4428** pulls past the elevator at Kief, N.D. on a rainy July day in 1993.

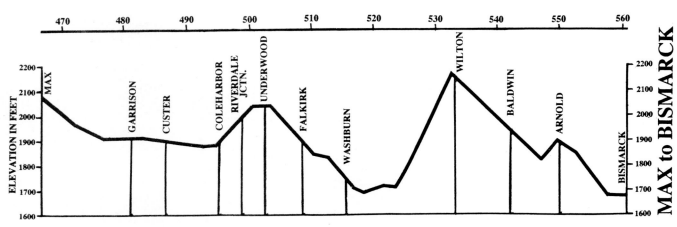

MAX to BISMARCK

the upper Missouri (the Sioux Ferry) is preserved here in Riverside Park.

Until Washburn, the Soo rather closely follows the Missouri River. Here, as the river comes in from the west, the line goes more northerly to Underwood, a town named after Fred Underwood who was at that time vice president of the Soo (1903); he was later to become president of the Eire Railroad. Soo facilities here included a water tank, a coaling derrick, and stockyards.

Coleharbor had a 24' x 80' depot, and stockyards. It should not be confused with the old abandoned Missouri River port town of Coal Harbor, which was 7 miles to the west. North from Coleharbor towards Garrison, the Soo tracks and US Highway 83 cross the impounded water of Lake Sakakawea. This lake—the longest lake in North Dakota, is the result of the Garrison Dam which was built during the late forties

and fifties to provide flood control along the Missouri River, hydroelectric power for the Bureau of Reclamation and recreation opportunities for tens of thousands of sportsmen. As Lake Sakakawea filled, it resulted in the impounding of many thousand acres of prime hunting areas in the Fort Berthold Indian Reservation.

As the waters started impounding behind the main dam, it became necessary to build a lengthy embankment across Snake Creek between Coleharbor and Garrison. This embankmant not only carries the Soo Line tracks but also U.S. Highway 83 which connects

TIMETABLE FROM 1937 SCHEDULE

ST. PAUL-MINNEAPOLIS
VIA DRAKE TO
MISSOURI RIVER DIVISION

		Miles	TIME TABLE 28				
	Ex.Su	Ex.Su			Ex.Su	Ex.Su	
......	† 9.00	† 1.10	0.0	Lv......Drake......Ar	†12.30	† 3.30	......
......	9.30	1.27	8.4	.........Klef.........	12.13	3.00	......
......	10.15	1.44	16.8	....Butte (Dogden)......	11.56	2.35	......
......	10.45	2.01	23.4	.......Kongsberg.........	11.40	2.01	......
......	11.23	2.17	30.2	.........Ituso.........	11.23	1.40	......
......	11.58	2.36	37.9	......Benedict.........	11.05	1.05	......
......	12.30	† 2.58	48.2	Ar.......Max......Lv	†10.45	†12.30	......
......	......	† 3.15	48.2	Lv.......Max......Ar	†10.00	......	......
......	......	3.45	59.3	.......Douglas........	9.30	......	......
......	......	4.20	68.3	.........Ryder........	8.50	......	......
......	......	4.45	74.7	.........Makoti........	8.10	......	......
......	......	5.00	79.7	Ar....Prairie Jct...Lv	† 7.35	......	......
......	† 6.50	† 5.00	79.7	Lv....Prairie Jct...Ar	7.35	5.35	......
......	7.05	5.10	83.6	Ar......Plaza......Lv	† 7.25	† 5.20	......
......	......	† 5.35	79.7	Lv....Prairie Jct...Ar	6.50		......
......	B W	5.45	83.4	.......Wabek.........	6.40	B W	......
......	Tue.	6.40	91.9	.......Parshall........	6.15	Mon.	......
......	Thu.	7.55	102.6	.....Van Hook........	5.30	Wed.	......
......	Sat.	7.40	112.1	Ar.....Sanish......Lv	† 5.00	Frl.	......
......	BY7.15	† 3.15	0.0	Lv.......Max......Ar	10.25	2.10	......
......	7.45	3.44	14.5	.......Garrison........	9.55	1.24	......
......	8.10	4.08	26.7	....Coleharbor........	9.28	12.25	......
......	9.10	4.24	34.0	....Underwood........	9.10	11.35	......
......	9.50	4.35	39.0	.......Falkirk.........	8.57	10.40	......
......	10.25	4.50	46.9	......Washburn........	8.41	10.15	......
......	11.45	5.29	64.2	.......Wilton.........	8.01	8.45	......
......	12.15	5.47	73.6	.......Baldwin........	7.40	7.40	......
......	f12.36	f 6.05	81.1	.......Arnold.........	f 7.23	f 7.00	......
......	1.10	6.30	91.7	Ar....Bismarck....Lv	† 7.00	AB6.30	......

AS C. M. St. P. & P. Ry. Station, Third Ave. S. and Washington.
BA Auto Stage connections to Plentywood.

* Daily. † Week days. ‡ Ex. Sat. ‖ Daily, except Mondays. f Flag stations.
‖ Meals. Light face type A. M. and black face type P. M. time.

Another Dam Mouth to Feed

Take a good look at that tunnel mouth in Garrison Dam, North Dakota. The Soo Line has to feed it, *and seven others,* thousands of tons of concrete required for lining. For each of these tunnels is approximately 1,200 feet long and they vary between 22 and 29 feet in diameter.
That's a lot of concrete!
But it's just a small part of

Garrison Dam—210 feet high, 12,000 feet long, 2,600 feet wide at the base and requiring 1,500,000 cubic yards of concrete.

Vast project, yes! But the Soo Line is up to the job—with a fleet of work-hungry giant diesel locomotives and a take-anything right-of-way leading straight to Riverdale Junction—just 14 miles from Garrison Dam.

Listen to the Railroad Hour every Monday evening on NBC

$OO $INE
—your working partner 7 days a week

FEBRUARY 1951

The Snow of 1951 was so deep at Riverdale that tunnels such as the one above were used to provide access to the switch stands.

Lawrence Draybus photo

Garrison depot in July 1970 shows the insulbrick siding that the Soo used extensively after World War II on many of its wooden structures.

Don Mahoney photo

Bismarck with Minot. This rolled earth embankment contains about 3,600,000 cubic yards of dirt, rock and gravel fill. Its total length is 20,000 feet with a maximum height of 85 feet. Although the Garrison Dam contains about 70,000,000 cubic yards of fill, this structure is nevertheless the second largest dam in the state of North Dakota. Besides carrying the roadway and tracks, it also provides secondary impoundment for the Garrison project.

The Garrison Diverson Act of 1944 promised irrigation waters for eastern North Dakota. However, the act has never been fully implemented and much of the impounded waters of Lake Sakakawea are used today to insure adequacy of river levels for barge traffic on the lower Missouri River.

Garrison (79 miles north from Bismarck) was named after Garrison Creek, so named because troops during the Fort Berthold days were garrisoned on its banks.

* * *

The following vignette was written by Don Mahoney, a sometime telegrapher and dispatcher of the Soo. It well illustrates one of many crises large and small handled by telegraphers on and off duty.

"In September of 1943 while employed as a station helper at Garrison, I was also a student telegrapher. I lived in the depot where I set up a folding bed next to the telegraph bay each night. About 3 a.m. on this particular night, I was awakened by an excited train crew who were pounding frantically on the bay windows. It was immediately obvious to me that there was a crisis as I awoke to see a steam locomotive standing in front of the depot with a lot of lights and people pounding on the windows. The crew informed me that they had been switching boxcar loads of grain in the yard at Max (15 miles north). They had kicked a string of

Lawrence Drabus

Normally a Congdon plow is a low maintenance bit of rolling stock. Air brakes occasionally go bum, however, and a plow will not move without repairs.

George Stancel

This 1948 view shows a quite different depot design than Soo Standard. Note the gold on black station sign.

eight cars into a siding fully expecting that they would roll to a stop. The rolling cars not only failed to stop, but rolled through a switch onto the main track and ran away. When this was discovered the entire crew jumped on the locomotive and started chasing the runaway cars. They had not been able to catch up in the fifteen miles to Garrison where they knew I was sleeping in the depot. They stopped and asked me to wire the dispatcher for instructions.

Because of the extreme grade variations in this area it was possible that the cars could cross over the grade and go on for miles or they might fail to climb the grade and come racing back in which case they would have wiped us all out. There was the additional threat of hitting cars at one of the many unprotected highway crossings along the way.

As a student telegrapher, it was true excitement and a real challenge to handle the communications as the dispatcher instructed the crew to proceed after the runaway cars and try to capture them, it was not long before they returned with the cars in tow. The cars had stopped on the crest of the grade just several miles south of Garrison."

Tales of Drake to Max to Bismarck and the New Town Line would be incomplete without an account of the life and times of Ira Toy, the Roadmaster at Drake.

Ira was born in little Albertsville, Wisconsin in 1908—at the age of 16, being quite muscular for his age, he went to work on the section gang for the Soo. During his first few days on the railroad he tamped ties barefooted. Seeing this, Roadmaster Ole Hoel bought Ira a pair of shoes and let him pay him back when he received his first pay check.

He worked his way up with steel gangs until he left the Steven's Point Gang in 1946 to become Roadmaster at Drake. This was just as the Soo was facing the formidible challenge of building the Garrison Dam. Ira had the single-handed charisma to keep his branch line 'up to snuff' to carry the dam material during those building years.

Courtney Brazel Collection

Between Garrison and Max in 1951: Conductor A.G. Olson at right in Checkered picket, at left Brakeman Smith. Ira Toy, Roadmaster, on top of snowbank.

James Welton photo

Ira Toy, the legendary roadmaster at Drake with his Fairmont speeder about 1952.

He took material from his brother roadmasters' supply at times and when accused of being a thief, his response was, "Well they say it takes one to know one!" With his dislike of paper work and going through channels, it was not uncommon for his superiors to find projects for which they were setting rush approval to be already done before official permission was received.

He was a family man with thirteen children (10 girls) and knew his Bible so well that he was sought after as a guest preacher many a time. Ira's district was tough snow country and a large portion of his winter's work was riding snow plows as plow operator.

Courtney Brazel (dispatcher at Enderlin) recalls that Ira wired him once from Washburn (where the track runs along the Missouri River) that muskrats were digging holes in the grade. The wire read, "I'm going to Bismarck to get a permit to shoot muskrats. So far I have got 19 of them."

Another time, Ira was running snowplow on the New Town Line and he crossed the dispatcher by requesting orders to go a different direction after the dispatcher had wired all the stations in the opposite direction to clear the line. When wired that he was going in the wrong direction, Ira's response was, "a wise man changes his mind–a fool never does."

Yes, Ira was one of those legends that made the Soo go as a family of dedicated railroaders, but his tremendous drive took its toll early; he died of a heart attack while working in his garden during the summer of 1957.

Drake became the rail center that Balfour aspired to be—its engine house was built in 1913. Max–466 miles west from Shoreham, is the junction for the New Town Subdivision. The Soo reached here in 1906—actually the town was three miles east and was moved to the railroad junction a year after the road was built. Although the Soo's officials in Minneapolis wished it named Junction City, local voices were loud enough that it came to be called just plain Max. (Actually Max was the name of the then postmaster's son).With railroad tracks running in four directions, the road had a two stall engine house, a wye, a standard 24' x 16' wooden tub water tower, a 20' wooden windmill on a 50' tower with a five horse-power Fairbanks–Morse engine pump, a coal dock with 15 buckets and a lorry, and a standard two story depot. This depot burned down in 1943 and was replaced with a rather unique two-story depot design.

Right: Note the absence of roof overhang on the 'new' Max depot. Looking west from the Highway 83 overpass; the tracks off in the distance go to New Town.

John Gjevre

Below: riprapping the Snake Creek embankment for the Soo tracks and Highway 83 between Coleharbor and Garrison (late 1950's).

Jerry Sahli

Above and to the right: views of the Benton packetboats tied up at the Soo Line's transfer elevator and coal chute along the Missouri at Washburn. A map of this installation along with another photo are found on page 114 *Part I.*

Both photos : Gordon Twedt Collection

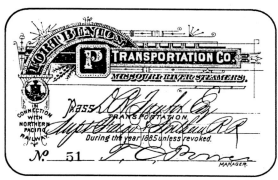

1885

New Town Line

Following the purchase of the Bismarck, Washburn and Great Falls Railway in 1904, management in Minneapolis felt it desireable to connect Bismarck with the main line and thus the line from Garrison to Max was built in 1906 and completed to Drake on the main line in 1909. As part of the same construction efforts in 1906, tracks were also laid west from Max in order to tap more of the rich bottomlands along the Missouri and to reach near to the Fort Berthold Indian Reservation.

Anticipating the railroad's coming, the community of Plaza was founded in July of 1906. However, Soo Line trains did not actually arrive until Thanksgiving Day of that same year. It was at that time the terminus of the Max line, although it would appear on current maps as if it had been constructed as a short branch off from Prairie Junction which is some three miles southeast. The actual location of Plaza was planned to be just outside the Fort Berthold Indian Reservation as the boundaries had been set by Congress in 1891. Actually, the Soo did traverse (in 1906) some eight miles or so over reservation land, perhaps not intentionally. This surveying 'error' was to be rectified in 1910 when Congress authorized additional lands of the Indian Reservation to be opened for settlement. Please see the full page advertisement on page 6 *Part I* for one example of how the railroad was to encourage new settlers and immigration into this area.

Old Soo Line maps show a proposed bridge across the Missouri and a hoped for extension into central Montana's Judith Basin. It now appears fortunate for the Soo that World War I and a general downturn in traffic had persuaded top brass of both the Soo and the Canadian Pacific not to follow the Milwaukee Road's rather futile westward expansion. From 1910 until 1914 the Soo waited patiently for Congress to authorize additional lands for settlement in the Fort Berthold Reservation. After the legal obstacles were cleared Soo tracks reached the 23.9 miles from Prairie Junction to Van Hook. The remaining 9 miles from Van Hook to Sanish were opened for traffic in 1915.

Because of regular flooding along the Missouri, some of this area was extremely fertile. It also was the very same land that was inundated following the

July 7, 1993   **Charles Bohi**

After spending the night at New Town, the crew 'caboose hops' back to Max where it will pick up some loads from the Washburn branch. Here, just out of New Town, it crosses a timber trestle that may have been built when the line was relocated during the Garrison Dam project.

construction of the Garrison Dam with the impoundment of Lake Sakakawea in 1952. Rising waters of the Missouri resulted in the flooding of two town sites. Buildings and businesses of Sanish and Van Hook were moved by the Bureau of Reclamation to New Town which today is the end of the branch.

Back in the early forties, when passenger traffic was common on the branch line mixed trains, a lady boarded at Sanish bound for Minot. She was very concerned that she make the connection at Max with the passenger train coming from Bismarck. She really became worried when the train stopped at Prairie Junction and she saw that the engine was starting to back up. She asked the brakeman why the delay and he replied that the engineer and the fireman had been fighting, "…the fireman had lost his pipe a couple miles back and the fireman had won the fight." Pretty soon the lady saw that the engine and train were backing up the branch as they were always scheduled to go to Plaza to pick up cream cans and unload some mail. The woman from Sanish by now was frantic and said she would buy the fireman a pipe. After a while the brakeman told her as the train moved forward again, "Everything is OK - the fireman got his pipe and we'll go ahead now." Of course the connection was made as scheduled with the northbound passenger train at Max . The poor lady never knew she had been the victim of a verbal practical joke.

*Soo Line **4427** and **735** westbound* with Harvey-New Town local at Max ND at 3 PM, May 22, 1984. Other than the two M of W gondolas, the train consisted of empty covered hoppers being dropped off at lineside elevators for grain loading.

Bob Wise

Dogden- named after nearby Dogden butte, a prominent 2291 foot peak that was a pioneer landmark. It was renamed Butte—just plain Butte, in 1927 because of post office confusion. This 1909 postcard view of a mixed train with Soo Standard 4-4-0 arriving from the east was taken only three years after the arrival of Soo rails.

Pete Bonesteel Collection

117

Gordon Twedt collection

Mixed train service was provided on the Sanish/Newtown Line into the 1960s, whereas pure passenger trains were seen through the 1920s. In 1919 it left Sanish at 6:30 a.m., and arrived in Plaza at 9:03 reaching Max just after 11 a.m. to connect with the Bismarck to Drake morning train. 1915 post card view of the two car accommodation at Plaza.

To the Right: 1915- a stray dog seems oblivious to the cameraman who was choosing to record the westbound way freight standing while the draymen unload incoming less than carload shipments. In 1990 Parshall's population was still over 900.

Al Ohrt collection

Minneapolis - December 21, 1944

TO ALL SECTION FOREMEN:

We recently had a case where a pair of wheels in a train were derailed and rerailed themselves without the knowledge of the trainman. The section foreman, in going over the track the following morning, observed signs of this derailment and reported the fact to this office. An investigation was started immediately to determine which car had been derailed and the car was found at a terminal approximately 100 miles distant with a large piece of the flange of the wheel broken out.

This wheel could have caused considerable damage to the rail and track, and could have caused an expensive and disastrous derailment.

When a section foreman observes conditions in going over his track which leads him to believe that a car has been derailed, of which he has received no report, he should immediately wire the Chief Dispatcher, the Roadmaster and the Chief Engineer, giving all the facts so that an investigation can be started immediately to determine what took place.

These instructions also apply when a section foreman observes signs or conditions which indicate that some object was dragging from the train or that there was defective equipment on the train which was causing damage to the rail or other track equipment. This report should be made by wire as soon as possible, so that the Chief Dispatcher may arrange to protect the train in case of defective equipment.

T.Z. Krumm

cc: Divn. Engrs.
    Roadmasters

Sanish: for thirty-seven years the terminus of the branch west from Max. Preliminary work had been started in 1915-16 to bridge the Missouri, but all plans for a westward extension of the Soo were scrapped during World War I. It is of interest that the Soo owned a stockyard on the west banks of the Missouri and before the building of the Four Bears bridge (above), cattle were driven to swim across the broad Missouri and to the loading pens in Sanish. From there the stockcars traveled over the Soo to the Twin Cities and the meat packing plants in South Saint Paul. Above photo circa 1940.

New Town: this townsite absorbed most of the former residents of Van Hook and Sanish as the waters of Lake Sakakawea rose.The first train arrived in New Town September 22, 1952. A one stall engine house and a turntable were built here as part of the Bureau of Reclamation's relocation efforts. At the close of the steam era Consolidation **451** was donated to the village by the Minneapolis,St. Paul and Sault Ste. Marie Railroad.

1970 photo by John Gjevre

1904 Ad for Soo Line Railroad

PLAZA: The original terminus of the line through Max in 1906 has an unusual (for North Dakota) town layout. The downtown is built around a central square or plaza (hence the name) much like Kenmare, Ryder and Columbus. The only other Soo town in North Dakota with a similar arrangement was the long defunct town of Imperial on the Flaxton branch. In the scene above can be seen a threshing machine, binders and a farm cook car as well as some teams. The livery barn stands with open door to the right. On the left can be seen cattle cars spotted east of the elevators; reminding us that this was and still is cow country in the Missouri breaks.

Douglas Wick Collection

1971 view of the now highly truncated depot at Plaza. Only the freighthouse remains, the agent's office and quarters and the passenger waiting rooms have been razed. At this point the depot still seems somewhat maintained, but not for too many more years.

Don Mahoney

2230A: a 1500 horsepower EMD F-7 that was delivered to the Wisconsin Central in August of 1953 is just seventeen years young as she balances on the New Town turntable before heading east with the golden fruit of North Dakota.

John Gjevre

**Grand Forks Daily Herald,
Tuesday, 29 September 1908.**

The new 40 horse power gasoline engine and ferry-boat at the crossing of the Missouri river south of Plaza has been put out of business already, so quick. This engine has quite a history. It was used on the Minnesota state fair grounds this year where it developed 70 horsepower. The Soo bought the engine for Mr. King, the ferryman, as the company was interested in getting the cattle west of the Missouri river to ship. They agreed to pay Mr. King 15 cents per head for ferrying the cattle across the river. Mr. King was attempting to do this with a light craft, whose heaviest timbers were made out of 2x4 with a 10 horsepower gasoline engine to propel the thing. This proved so slow that it was decided to get a heavier engine and make better time. The Soo went good for the engine and other necessary material and besides sent up several gasoline experts to help install the engine. The engine was hurried up from St. Paul and a train was sent out from Drake a week ago Sunday with the sole object of getting this engine to Plaza in the quickest time possible. While Mr. King was at Plaza to get the new engine, some of his subordinates who were running the light craft on the Missouri river struck a rock with the propeller of the boat and knocked it into a hundred pieces. Just at that time Manager Keho got new light as to getting cattle across the Missouri river and commenced swimming them across. The river is half a mile wide and the cattle were driven out on a sandbar and then they were forced to swim the channel which is not more than a couple of rods wide. The first time the cattle were forced to cross they not only swam across the channel but also swam back again. After seeing how easy it was to get cattle across the river, 1100 head of Mr. Phalen's cattle were driven across in one day. Any old cowboy would have swam them across in the first place, but the old time cowboy is a thing of the past and only occasionally strays around to give the tenderfoot pointers that are of value to him as in this case. The ferry boat is a derilict so far as ferrying cattle is concerned and the Soo went to a lot of needless expense.

John Gjevre photo

1970- a short freight makes quick time past Ryder's standard two story second class depot. Ryder had been founded in 1903 and was originally called Centerville. This name, however, was considered unacceptable by the postal service. When the postal inspector came to the community, he had borrowed a warm buffalo coat from Arthur F. Ryder (of Minot). Because the weather was so cold, the postal inspector named Centerville— Ryder as a 'thank you' to the man who had loaned him the warm coat.

Gordon Twedt collection

DOUGLAS, 11 miles west of Max, was the first town on the branch. This 1914 photo shows George Burgerson with his distallate Oil Pull hauling twelve wagon loads of grain to market.

Below: January 1982 specialized vehicles for a special railroad wear the white and red at Shoreham

Soo Line Railroad

Soo Line Railroad

One of several distinctive Soo trademarks started as a marketing tool in August 1963 when the Colormark program was introduced. These distinctive cars had a white (light grey) body with a large panel or door painted either red, blue or green. All cars in the Colormark program were custom fitted for specific shipping uses. Cars designed to carry a select variety of goods were designated with a red band or a red door. Cars designed for a single type of load were coded green. Finally, cars designed for moving commodities in bulk were coded blue (such as grain hoppers).

The covered gondola 68289 was one of an order of fifteen 52' gondolas built by Thrall Car Company in 1968.

Soo-owned tanker for fuel oil haulage 6-29-64.

Lloyd Berger, Jr.

Richard Logan

Above: a tender was a most specialized car. These were not the victims of planned obsolescence but rather of technological advances and economics.

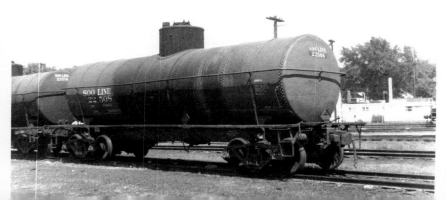

Richard Yaremko

758, 568 at Foxholm, ND September 1977. Northwest of Minot on the Soo main to Portal—it was the scene of a lynching in the early days when vigilantes hanged a man on the Soo stockyard gate. Its name came from Foxholm, England, but there were few English who settled here.

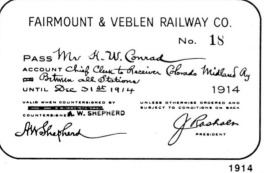

Robert Kjelland

Above: **4648**–an ex-Milwaukee GP 40-2 has been repainted into the red, white and black and equipped with ditch lights. It heads a long lashup at Valley City. February 1991.

Left: Soo utility truck (Chevrolet) at Harvey 3-28-81. Like many modern businesses, many company vehicles, most locomotives and rolling stock of the Soo have been subject to lease arrangements.

Richard Logan

Daryl Thompson Collection

Fairmount, North Dakota Soo Depot built by the Minneapolis and Pacific in 1887 and replaced by a more conventional MS & PSSM depot. It is only 20' wide compared to the more standard 24' of Soo and CP depots. Mr. Ballard is on the right and to the left is Russ Gordon. Note the Fairbanks-Morse platform scale at right. (circa 1912).

Standard First Class depot at Fairmount on September 15, 1970 looking west towards the Miller Brothers' grain complex.

Walter Evans

The Fairmount And Veblen Railway

The story of this branch has been detailed in *Part I* pp 120-124. Briefly, its origins can be traced to local farmers' attempts to have a railroad to serve this gently rolling land at the very southernmost portion of the Red River Valley. Northeastern South Dakota had been opened for general settlement as the Sioux Indians were pushed into reservation lands up in the *Coteau du Prairie* (the Sisseton or Veblen Hills) during the late 1880s. Between 1900 and 1907 Anton Dahl and others tried to get funding for a railroad to connect the Soo with Veblen, a well established inland town at the foot of the Coteau hills. Their dream was to languish until 1913 when Julius Rosholt, a Wisconsin entrepeneur, was able to construct the line as far as Veblen. The Fairmount and Veblen Railway was extended up into the Coteau hills the following year. The Soo Line was to purchase the road in 1915. This area had been settled mainly by families of Scandinavian, German and Luxemburgish descent. The towns of Rosholt, New Effington and Claire City were all started in the grain fields during the fall of 1913; F. E. Sprout was in charge of developing these townsites. The railroad had its headquarters with its own most distinctive depot in Fairmount. By the early

To the right is a rare photo of the Fairmount & Veblen's Fairmount depot. Julius Rosholt, the line president, must have liked gables, for there are four. Also of interest is that from 1913 to 1916, there were four depots for four different railroads in Fairmount.

**1915 Postcard view:
Pete Bonesteel Collection**

Below: Fairmount roundhouse during the twenties. This structure was built in 1916 to replace the Fairmount and Veblen Railway enginehouse which was torn down by Soo crews. The coal derrick at Fairmount from the F & V was dismantled in 1951.

Stuart J. Nelson Collection

FAIRMOUNT & VEBLEN DEPOT.
FAIRMOUNT · N·D·

1920s the Soo Line serviced this branch out of its Hankinson terminal.

Rosholt has been the most durable of the towns that developed along the old F and V. In 1994 it still has a primary and secondary school, a modern nursing home, a lovely park, an area museum (housed in the original 1913 depot which has been authentically maintained) as well as a large farmers' cooperative elevator which ships out dozens of unit grain trains annually.

Fairmount and Veblen Railway Marshalling yard 1914. That's 'Doc' Strait at the door.
Daryl Thompson

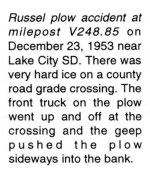

Russel plow accident at milepost V248.85 on December 23, 1953 near Lake City SD. There was very hard ice on a county road grade crossing. The front truck on the plow went up and off at the crossing and the geep pushed the plow sideways into the bank.

William Egan Jr.

At home on the Coteau Hills. Amidst big hills on a great South Dakota prairie, **717** appears at Grenville (9-3-52). For many, these were better, simpler days.

Bruce Black

During the steam era, Veblen had its original 24' x 60' depot to which a 20 foot extension was added in 1920. There also was the customary section house, a two stall 40' x 81' x 20' engine house (retired in 1955), a 24' x 40' machine shop, a coal derrick, a water tank, an oil house, a sand bin and a stock yard. Grenville at line's end had a one stall engine house, a tank and windmill, a coal platform and a stockyard in addition to its depot. Since there was no hotel in Grenville, the trainmen would sleep in a small boxcar shed here after they had tied up for the night. The crew brought their own sheets and blankets.

New Effington also had a windmill and tank and likewise there was a mill and tank at milepost 197.9. The extension up into the Coteau hills was circuitous and steep and really generated little traffic since much of the Coteau is rocky and more fit for cattle grazing than farming. Deep clear lakes abound in this region and Seche Hollow, a naturalist paradise near Veblen, has managed to retain much of its pristine character even though South Dakota has made it into a state park. Unfortunately for the F and V and the Soo, the recreational wonders never generated traffic and the line from Veblen to Grenville was abandoned in 1971.

1913 Fairmount and Veblen passenger service inaugural waiting to board at Fairmount. This line, orignially to Veblen and later extended to Grenville, South Dakota, was built to Soo Line specifications and was purchased by the Soo in 1915. The line still has service to Veblen and indeed the Rosholt (SD) elevator is one of the larger shippers of unit grain trains on the Soo.

Right: 1917 postcard view of Rosholt with its classic F & V depot. This depot has been moved up the hill to the highway across from the highschool and is well-restored and serving as the village musuem.

Jeanne Swartz Collection

Below: Builders' photo of an H-1 light Pacific. There were 22 engines in this class; all were built by Alco's Schenectady's works (1904-1907).

Lawrence Draybus Collection

Depot and Elevators Rosholt, S.D.

Wishek Sub

Hankinson was founded in 1896 as both the Soo and Jim Hill's Great Northern were in their ongoing battle for supremacy in the wheat country (see page 16 *Saga of the Soo Part I*). Much railroad activity was centered in Hankinson for crews based here serviced the Fairmount and Veblen branch into South Dakota and the Coteau Hills as well as the Bismarck extension westward to Wishek. The Hankinson yard boasted a four stall engine house and a seventy foot turntable. The Soo did not have a well here and consequently water service for steam was provided by the city. It is going west at Hankinson that Soo rails split with the original main line of the Minneapolis and Pacific (Bismarck extension). The mainline that was constructed during 1891-93 went northwest out of Hankinson to Portal and the Canadian Pacific connection via Enderlin, Valley City, Harvey, Minot and Kenmare. After about 1920, the Fairmount and Veblen (Grenville) line was serviced out of the Hankinson roundhouse. That line was constructed in 1913 as the Fairmount and Veblen Railway and purchased by the Soo Line in 1915.

Digressing, just a bit regards Hankinson; it was founded by Richard Henry Hankinson, a Civil War veteran who was the first promoter of the telephone in the State of Minnesota. By 1878, just two years after the invention of the telephone by Bell, Hankinson had ten subscribers in Minneapolis including the Pillsbury Mills. In 1881 Hankinson moved his family to an area south of present Hankinson in Dakota Territory and started farming there. Soo tracks came north of his acres in 1886 and Hankinson then developed the townsite which bears his name. With his expertise in communications it is not surprising that he was to build all the telegraph line for the Soo west of the Red River in the 1880's and 1890's. Hankinson died in 1911 of cancer of the stomach.

Views above and below of Ransom (circa 1900). The Soo had a water tower and a coal dock here, but by 1915 most of the town had disappeared.

Both photos from James Fischer Collection.

Travelling westward from Hankinson, a crew member looking south from Soo tracks will see a high dune (150 feet high) known as Lightning's Nest. The hills of the Dovre Morraine form a prominent range to the south and west. Four miles west of Hankinson the tracks ascend the shoreline of ancient Lake Agassiz (which today forms the floor of the Red River Valley of the North). The Dovre Morraine lies about two miles south of the Soo tracks and parallels the road westward for almost 25 miles.

Lidgerwood (1990 population 799) was named for the Minneapolis and Pacific Railway's right-of-way agent, George L. Lidgerwood. Lidgerwood, like so many other North Dakota communities, is famous for its exports. People exported include Chester Fritz, a Far East financier, benafactor and philanthropist, and 'Spike' Movius, President Eisenhower's ghost writer.

Continuing west, tracks cross the Wild Rice River and then ascend the Dovre Morraine. There is a continual grade from Ransom all the way to the town of Nicholson, near the western shore of ancient Lake Sargeant.

Oakes was platted by the Western Town Lot Company as the rails of the Northern Pacific reached the Chicago Northwestern Line which had been building up from Columbia, South Dakota in 1886. Minneapolis and Pacific rails reached Oakes the following year. At the turn of the century Oakes could boast of eight passenger trains as well as eight freights scheduled each day. Soo Line facilities here included a three stall roundhouse with a 56 foot turntable, a wood water tank and a derrick type coaling station, in addition to the interchange with the Chicago and Northwestern and Northern Pacific. For more than thirty years the North American Creamery plant at Oakes provided significant inbound and outboud traffic. Even today this community can boast that it has more

Eugene Simek Collection

Fullerton was laid out along the Minneapolis and Pacific Railway in 1887 on land donated by Edwin Sweet who later became a Congressman in Michigan. Its name came from Sweet's wife's maiden name which was Fuller. The above photo shows Fullerton's 24 foot wide depot in 1914. Destroyed by fire in 1915, it was replaced with a standard Soo two story 2nd class depot in December of 1915. Fullerton also had a water tank and windmill.

rail lines entering it than any other North Dakota community. Even though Soo Line service terminates at Oakes in 1995, Soo-owned rails continue westward with service being provided by lessee Dakota and Missouri Valley Railroad. Just to the west of Oakes, Soo tracks again traverse a dry lake bottom (old Lake Dakota) through which the James River flows south.

Eighty-two miles west of Hankinson, the branch of the Milwaukee Road is crossed and then the rails climb a rather stiff grade (from Merricourt, altitude 1644 feet to Kulm, altitude 1966 feet, in only twelve miles) towards the top of the Missouri Plateau.

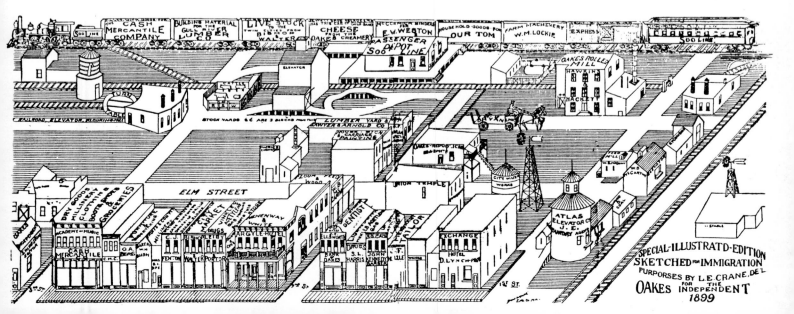

Wishek's depot in 1915 was the classic two story Soo Standard. After being destroyed by fire, the Soo elected to use the cement block beanery. This area was settled in the late 1800's by German-Russians and even 100 years later, German is commonly spoken. The cement block depot is pictured on page 108 of *Part I*.

Agent William T. Kenady, Sr. is seated with his son, William Jr. standing next to the stove. Kenady Sr. hired out as agent with the Soo at Lehr in 1909 and moved to Parshall during the land rush to the Fort Berthold Reservation (see page 6 *Part I*). While in Parshall, he also homesteaded and his family lived in a claim shanty in order to prove up the land. He served as agent at Cogswell, Plaza, Ashley and Rockford (MN). His son attended college with a latin major, but found lifelong employment as a depot agent with the Great Northern (like many depot-dwelling sons, for whom the telegraph sounder provided railroad music at an early age).

Although the Soo laid rails from Boynton to Kulm in 1892, it waited until 1898 to reach Wishek. This town was named for J. H. Wishek, who had been instrumental in securing right-of-way for the railroad in McIntosh county.

Wishek (137 miles west of Hankinson) is at 2010' with many steep hills and valleys. Fortunately, Soo surveyors chose to locate the line in an old drainage channel from the Altamont Morraine to the Missouri River, eliminating a great deal of cuts and fills. At Wishek, an eight stall roundhouse had been built with a sixty foot turntable (installed in 1907). Wishek's standard two-story depot was replaced with the cement block depot (pictured in *Part I*, page 108), which had originally been constructed as a crew bunkhouse and beanery. Wishek had a 64' 192' stockyard—much larger than usual, but then this entire area was, and continues to be devoted to both ranching and farming.

The line to Ashley goes at the bottom of one of the old drainage or river channels, and Ashley is remarkable in that it stands on a level plain of about six square miles. Continuing northwest to Napoleon, the grade slants downwards as the rails must reach towards the Missouri River at Bismarck (elevation 1670').

Thomas Lowry, the streetcar rapid transit magnate of Minneapolis and Saint Paul, had been instrumental earlier in developing the Aberdeen, Bismarck

Interior of Cogswell depot circa 1926. The coal burning stove, pencil sharpener, filing racks, cubby holes, typewriter and adding machine all add up to purposeful clutter.

OT AND ELEVATORS
BRADDOCK N.D.

Inset: the same station in 1942 shows that a window has been added for ventilation. Note the postal telegraph sign. Although Wisconsin Central lines used Western Union telegraph, the Soo Line did not receive Western Union telegraph services until the War Years.

Douglas Wick Collection

Above: Scene of Braddock circa 1916 showing two elevators and the flour mill. An early Ford Runabout is waiting for its passenger.

Collection of George Stancel

This photo of Braddock depicts town life centering about the station in its heyday. Note the 'steamer trunks' and sample cases. I suspect the hatted man on the left to be a 'drummer.' One should note the trees to the left and compare this with the 1942 view of the depot which shows not only a more developed community, but also a run down community. Braddock's peak population was 216 in 1920

Chales W. Bohi

Western Division Timetable #1, from May 7, 1961, contained this special instruction: "All trains approach Ashley at restricted speed as main track switch may be lined for Aberdeen Main." This note came about as a result of a grade built by a Soo Line predecessor from Aberdeen, S.D. to Bismarck, N.D. The company built track on that grade from Ashley to the North Dakota capital. While little evidence exists to indicate that the Soo Line ever intended to lay rail to Aberdeen, it is interesting to note that the front of the 'Second Class' depot at Ashley faces the 'Aberdeen Main,' while the rear faces the Pollock Line. By 1972, all dreams of extensions were long gone, and the switch of what might have been a prairie junction is set for the branch to Pollock.

and Northwestern Railway (see page 17 *Part I*). Although that railway was never built, the 210 miles from Aberdeen to Bismarck were graded, and the Soo did make use of the grade for its rails from Ashley to Bismarck.

Lowry had purchased land in speculation that the Soo's coming would cause property values to rise in North Dakota's capital, but the Soo, under Edmund Pennington, and Underwood had priorities elsewhere, much to the distress of farmers along this frontier, as well as the Bismarck newspapers. The distress was so great in fact, that James W. Foley of the *Bismarck Tribune* penned these lines describing how distressing the repeated postponments were for the folk of Emmons and Logan counties. The Soo finally reached Burleigh County and Bismarck in 1902.

Waiting for the Soo

By James W. Foley

A farmer once sat by the grade of the Soo,
And waited and waited and waited
In vain for the trains which were soon to pass through
As stated, oft stated, oft stated.
In storm and in blizzard, in sunshine and rain,
He watched, while the gophers were eating his grain,
But years passed away, and his vigil was in vain,
Yet he waited, and waited, and waited.

The seasons passed out and the seasons came in,
While he waited, and waited, and waited.
He grew pale, faint and weary, and sunburned and thin,
Yet he hated, he hated, he hated
To give up his place by the side of the grade,
Which ages before his forefathers had made,
For he felt that the steel rails were soon to be laid,
So he waited, and waited, and waited.

His hair it grew long, and his beard it grew white,
While he waited, and waited, and waited.
Yet he watched through the daytime and watched all the night,
And waited, and waited, and waited.
His farm buildings crumbled and went to decay.
The angel of death took his neighbors away,
But he laughed and said, "Gabe, I have come here to stay."
And he stay did, and stay did, and stay did.

Years, ages, and centuries 'round him had rolled;
Yet he waited, and waited, and waited;
The last trump had blown and the last bell had tolled,
Yet he waited, and waited, and waited.
Then Gabriel, thinking he hadn't quite heard,
Blew a second long blast, and then even a third;
But the farmer grinned grimly and never once stirred,
Just waited, and waited, and waited.

Then Gabriel came from his station on high,
And pray did, and pray did, and pray did.
"Now, Gabe," said the farmer, "that's all in your eye,"
And he waited, and waited, and waited.
"My dear sir," said Gabe, "you'll be left all alone;"
"You're wasting your breath, for I'm deaf as a stone,"
Said the farmer, and Gabe gave an audible groan
And waited, and waited, and waited.
*   *   *   ***
A million years passed by, and still the two stayed
And waited, and waited, and waited.
One day a shrill whistle they heard up the grade,
Yes they did, yes they did, yes they did.
"What's that?" gasped the farmer, and Gabe's wonder grew.
"It's Adam the Second," said Gabe. "If it's true,"
Said the farmer, "I'll bet you he's bringing the Soo,"
And he fainted, and fainted, and fainted.

Dry Lake
near Ashley, N. Dak.
March 27, 1945

Jim Fischer Collection

The line south from Wishek to Pollock, South Dakota (POLLOCK SUB) was remarkable during construction in 1901 in that it was built right through a dry lake bed between Ashley and Danzig about one-third of a mile from the west shoreline; all was well for 44 years.

During the spring runoff of 1945 the lake filled with water and a decision was made to abandon the original line and a new road bed was prepared some two miles to the east.

At the same time that the new line was being so remarkably graded, the track and ties floated up from the underwater roadbed and the free floating track began drifting to and fro in the lake.

It was then that Roadmaster Charles Hayes fashioned a motorized raft from a speeder car. Using winches and cable he was able to push a 600 foot section to the east shore where the rails were salvaged and relaid on the newly prepared roadbed detouring the eastern shore. Additional sections of the track sank (in twelve feet of water) and carefully the locations were marked. The following winter, Hayes returned with a crawler tractor and grappling hooks and salvaged another 700 feet of track through the ice. The photo to the left shows what the Soo Line Navy's SeaBees encountered during the summer of '45.

INFORMATION ABOUT THE
HOMESTEAD LAW

1. Any person who is not the owner of more than 160 acres of land in any state or territory can acquire land under the homestead law. He need not be a full citizen of the United States.

2. A man has to be twenty-one years of age to make a homestead entry, unless he is married or the head of a family.

3. A married woman has no right to make a homestead entry, but a deserted wife can make a homestead entry.

4. A single woman over the age of twenty-one years has the right to make a homestead entry.

5. A single woman does not forfeit her homestead entry by marriage, if thereafter she continues to comply with the laws as to residence, improvements and cultivation. But a husband and wife cannot both hold separate homestead entries and prove up both.

6. The widow or children of a homesteader are not required to reside on their homestead after his death, but must continue cultivation by agent or otherwise. The widow can enter a homestead in her own right while cultivating that of her deceased husband, in which event she must actually reside on the land entered in her own name.

7. Homestead entries cannot be made for more than 160 acres of land.

8. Five years' residence from the date of entry is required on the homestead for perfecting the title, except that sailors or soldiers of the late war may apply, as time of residence, the period of their military service; but in all cases there must not be less than one years' actual residence on and improvement of the land.

9. After fourteen months' residence on a homestead the entry may be commuted, if desired, by paying $1.25 per acre, and the government will then give patent.

10. A person who entered less than 160 acres of land as a homestead before March 1, 1889, may now enter enough additional land which, added to the amount originally entered, will not exceed 160 acres.

11. A person who has not perfected title to a homestead entry which he made prior to June 5, 1900, may make a new homestead entry of 160 acres regardless of his previous filing.

12. Any person, who prior to June 5, 1900, commuted a homestead entry, may now take another homestead, but must reside on it five years. He cannot commute an entry again.

13. It is necessary to appear in person when making an entry of homestead lands.

14. Land office fees, when application is made for homestead entry, are as follows: $14 for 160 acres; $13 for 120 acres; $7 for 80 acres; $6 for 40 acres.

The following is from the introduction for a mid twenties <u>Soo Line Settlers' Guide to North Dakota</u>

Introduction

Less than a generation ago North Dakota was government homestead land. A beneficent government gave to every citizen, without regard to previous profession, calling or trade, an equal right to file on a homestead.

The lure of "free land" attracted to this State, the same as it had done to every other State in its early history, people from every walk of life. Many who came were experienced farmers, and their fine farms, well equipped with substantial buildings, are evidence of the success and prosperity they are enjoying. Large numbers remained only long enough to "prove up", sell out and go back to their old occupations. Land became cheap as these "adventurers" moved out. The result was that large tracts of former homesteads were bought up and the owners developed what was known as the "bonanza wheat farms" some of them thousands of acres in extent. The fertile soil was the richest wheat land in the world. Wheat is the greatest crop for the pioneer farmer. It is easily grown with limited capital and machinery. Seeded early in the spring, it requires no further attention until harvest time. North Dakota soon attained the reputation of being the greatest spring wheat State in the Union.

Today, as a result of the cropping of wheat year after year on the same ground, the yield per acre has been reduced to such an extent that many farmers are producing their grain at a loss. Those who do not practice a proper rotation of crops, or diversification are being forced out of business.

The big grain farms are now being cut into smaller farms, and the farmer who is practicing a diversified system of farming and raising livestock has no worries as to the future.

That North Dakota is rapidly changing its method of farming is evidenced by the great increase of dairy farming in the last few years. North Dakota farmers purchased a thousand head of dairy cattle from Wisconsin in 1923.

North Dakota is at the threshold of a great era of substantial agricultural development. The State has never had a "land boom". Due to the change in farming methods which is resulting in "grain miners" moving to other localities, it has an abundance of good fertile land, which can be acquired now for the lowest price it will ever be purchased.

A study of the following pages will convince one beyond a doubt that North Dakota is a good State in which to make a home and prosper. Its lands will produce crops the equal of any other State in the Northwest, with proper and intelligent treatment.

The Minneapolis, St. Paul and Sault Ste. Marie Railway Company has no lands for sale in North Dakota. Its management does believe that there are great possibilities for agriculture in North Dakota, and its services are at your disposal to find a new farm home in that state.

H. S. FUNSTON
Land Commissioner
The Soo Line

At the time the above was written, it basically contained no untruths. Changes the author could have never foretold were to come with the drought and depression of the thirties which catastrophically starved a great percentage of the state's farmers. With World War II, many of the marginal farmers went to the defense industries, never to return. The total mechanization of mid-American farming which accelerated rapidly after the War was to make diversification an obstacle rather than a means to prosperity. Today, profitable farming is best done by a family unit, but it is heavily capitalized, generally only mildly diversified and demands huge energy imput in terms of machine fuel, fertilizer and chemicals. The railroad's early hopes of having the two way haul—

grain and cattle to the population centers for consumption and manufactured goods and supplies back to the rural areas for the most part does not exist today. With larger and more efficient farms, the towns and villages have necessarily become smaller—some to vanish altogether. Trucks, motor cars and the information superhighway have advantaged the Dakota and Midwestern farmers in many cases to a life style and degree of sophistication that is the envy of many a city brother.

The Soo Line and Immigration

By Father William Sherman

The Soo Line began in the minds of it's Minneapolis merchant organizers as a vehicle to bring agricultural produce to and from the Twin Cities. Its goal was local and regional trade. As construction continued through Wisconsin and Michigan and into the Dakotas, and as the various mergers took place, the Soo's management never seemed to lose sight of their early intent. Even the 1888, 1893 and 1904 connections with the Canadian Pacific did not radically change its early woodland and granger role. Unlike the Northern Pacific, the Great Northern and the Milwaukee, the Soo never, for example, made a serious effort at stimulating an influx of settlers from the old country. Those larger and more flamboyant rival railroads had enjoyed the advantage, in this regard, of being on the Great Plains a decade before the Soo tracks were laid. Before and after the turn of the century these three giants distributed literally millions of pieces of literature throughout Britain, Scandinavia and the German countries. In much of Western Europe they had agents in place soliciting movement across their lines to America's West. The Soo, in contrast, focused its eyes primarily on the matter of grain and merchandise. It never called itself an 'empire builder.'

As a result, no sizeable portion of the Dakotas can be classed as the product of Soo railroad promotional schemes. The Milwaukee brought masses of German-Russians to northern South Dakota and southcentral North Dakota. The Great Northern claims credit for fashioning the decidedly Norwegian counties in northwestern North Dakota. The Northern Pacific cast its patterns of settlements from Fargo through to the Montana line and well beyond. The Soo Line (with more limited aspirations) built 'wheat lines' not ethnic empires.

Yet the Soo did have settlement in mind as a secondary goal. It focused, at least in certain time periods, on the task of bringing American residents from eastern states to what undeveloped lands were along its trackage. We know that from 1903 to 1915 under the guidance of general land agent, D.W. Casseday, the line advertised both in English language newspapers and in a number of foreign language American publications. The Soo urged settlers to come via its rail conveyances to what the Swedes called 'Norra Dakota och Södra Dakota' to what the Germans termed as 'Nord und Süd Dakota' and what the Norwegians termed 'Nord og Syd Dakota.' In English the Dakotas were called the 'Golden Grain Belt.' State and provincial immigration agencies got into the act during those same early-in-the-century decades. Northern Michigan, the Canadian Prairie Provinces and even Oregon and Washington were portrayed in the Scandinavian and German languages as the sources for cheap land. State literature boasted that fruitful acreages could be found all along the Soo and its connected lines.

And indeed, settlers responded, dropping off at the newly founded townsites, choosing what new land remained or occupying farms left by disillusioned homesteaders. No doubt hundreds of western American families today will find, as they trace their family tree, a mention of Soo Line accomodations which brought them to their original farmsteads. It is of historic interest that the bankers, lawyers and a majority of the business men in those early frontier towns were yankees who had moved to the west of America in search of a more rewarding life than was possible in Massachusetts or Ohio.

There is a region northwest of Minot, however, where the Soo Line can be shown to have exerted pioneer settlement force. The Soo tracks on to Portal were laid through virgin ranching territory. Foxholm, Donnybrook, Kenmare and Bowbells all saw Soo rails reach them in 1893. (Jimmy Buzzell, a section foreman, built the first structure in Bowbells.) The Federal Land

1898

Surveyors came two years later and very soon the railroad gave its agent, Frank Swickard, the task of enticing settlers to this region. Through his efforts a group of German Baptists (called Dunkards) came from Indiana. Transportation was free to those who chose land. The Burke County History says cars were sidetracked and used for housing, stables and temporary storage. Later the Soo built two structures, 16 x 100 feet in size, partioned off to provide room for those waiting until their claim shanties were complete.

Soo Line records concerning these promotion activities are scarce. Although it is hard to determine where this sort of settler assistance occurred, it is certain that some variation of these efforts took place elsewhere, at least on a small scale. North Dakota newspapers reported in October, 1915, for instance, that fourteen carloads of immigrant goods moved through Minot, destined for Tolley. Also on the train was an 'accommodation car' for families which included sleeping and cooking facilities. Those particular settlers came from eastern Iowa and western Illinois. News reports at that time said the Soo Line "began the work of immigration in this area about two years ago." The railroad spent $20,000 during 1914 in "getting settlers interested in lands along its line in the state (of North Dakota)."

Americans (English speaking yankees) and others from a number of states, moved aggressively into that area between Minot and Portal. Even today this is a portion of the West which can still be described as 'Soo Territory.'

The Burke County endeavours concentrated mainly on enticing eastern settlers to the West. But this is not to say that the Soo Line was hostile to foreign speaking immigrants. In fact a case can be made that the officials were surprisingly sympathetic. A look at the names given to townsites along the various rail lines would seem to say that officials on the Great Northern and Northern Pacific were oblivious to the ethnic concerns for those who would take their adjacent farmsteads. Only a few of the over one hundred towns along their main lines through North Dakota have a Germanic or Scandinavian name (Bismarck was named to impress German investors in the Northern Pacific and we find Bremen, Hamburg and Karlsruhe on the Great Northern's 'Surrey Cutoff'). And this, in spite of the fact that, perhaps over 70 percent of the state's settlers would be of that set of national backgrounds. The truth is that Yankee and British names proliferated along those routes as they moved from Minnesota to Montana.[1]

The Soo Line indeed had its share of Yankee and Anglo names–the owners and directors were of that background–but Soo officials seemed to go out of their way to accommodate the 'foreigners.' Thus we find in the Ukranian area of central North Dakota such towns a Ruso and Kief. The German Russians further south have Kulm, Lehr, Danzig and Wishek. On the Chippewa reservation in western Minnesota towns such as Mahnomen, Ogema and Waubun flourish. North Dakota Mandans have their Makoti, while the North Dakota French-Indians have their hero, Joseph Rollette, memorialized in the Turtle Mountain area town by the same name. So also their missionary priest, Father John Malo is remembered by the village of Mylo. The Irish have their moment in the sun (or green) with echos of the 'Old Sod' in towns like Kensal, Kenmare and Donnybrook. The Finnish settlement in Nelson County is named Pelto (Finnish for plowed land). The happy Danes have Alsen on the Wheat Line while the Swedes have Karlstad and Strandquist in northwestern Minnesota. Their Norsk neighbours have Oslo, Viking, Newfolden and Bergen (ND). As if to satisfy the United Nations in North Dakota the Poles had Poland, then there is Lucca (Italian), Venturia and Cuba (Spanish), Napoleon and Bordulac (French), and even Cathay (Chinese).

Bringing foreign-born Americans to the new lands happened in other ways than name choices. Unwittingly, perhaps, the Soo Line allowed immigrants to see the West through employment procedures. For decades the work crews dotting the prairies were usually made up of unskilled 'off-the-boat' laboring men. The Soo Line policy was to use contractors to grade and prepare the roadbed. These firms tended to hire local help as much as possible -- townfolk and farmers used their own teams for the grading, ditching and filling. In 1905, for instance, Winston Brothers (of Minneapolis) had 1000 teams and 2000 individuals at work near Kenmare. (The term 'individuals' is used advisedly, for women, too, were laboring side by side with the men. Catherine Fettig, for example, a 16 year old girl of Russian birth was on a crew as a grade was prepared in central Pierce County). It needs to be mentioned that this summer railroad work opportunity was crucial to many foreign and American homesteaders as they struggled to

[1] In order to be fair; Gascoyne on the Milwaukee main line honors a French construction foreman. The Milwaukee also had Hague, Strasburg and Zeeland on a branch line.

Havana on the adandoned Great Northern branch was named for Havana, Illinois–not Cuba, but a Munich and Pekin can be found on Great Northern branches and Berlin is to be found on a Northern Pacific branch.

get safely through the first years of life on the remote prairies. Then too, some of these pioneers would travel to Minnesota or Wisconsin during the winter months to work in logging and lumbering trying to earn dollars for an additional cow or extra horse or perhaps a walking plow or drill.

Upon completion of the roadbed and bridges the Soo moved in with its own track laying gangs, complete with bunk cars, cook cars and rail and tie facilities. (See the description of this organization on pages 22-24 *Saga of the Soo Part I*). Workers on these crews were recruited for the season from eastern cities, and were for the most part newly arrived foreigners. Thus it came about that literally thousands of newcomers saw western opportunities first hand while driving spikes and tamping ties. Most would return to those large cities, but some remained in the west as section employees; some, records tell us, became farmers.

It wasn't construction activities alone that brought 'foreign speaking' immigrants to the Soo areas of the west. Improvments, maintenance, roundhouse and yard facilities demanded a constant supply of working folk. Just a sample of 1910 Census records shows what took place each year along Soo Line tracks. McHenry County, North Dakota - in April that year six Italian born men were at Balfour; all were classed as R.R. laborers. Twenty miles away at Velva, there were five Greek men who had arrived in the U.S. in 1909 and 1910. Only two spoke English; all were unmarried and none had filed papers for citizenship.

Another example - during 1910 at the Soo town of Wishek, there were eleven Greeks listed as 'R.R. laborers,' all were single, all had immigrated between 1907 and 1910 and none had yet sought citizenship. Wishek also had four German-Russian section workers and a Swedish-born section foreman. The 'R.R. shops' classification listed thirteen U.S. born men, but one each of Bulgarian, Swedish and Norwegian birth. A Russian-born Jew was a 'fireman-foreman.'

Enderlin in spring, 1910 had by census count, six German-born section workers all married, all of whom had arrived between 1907-1909. Also present was a crew of seven Greek-born section workers; none could speak English, all came to the States between 1907 and 1909. Their ages were from 20 to 35 and none had applied for citizenship. Enderlin had 15 other individuals of Greek-birth working in various capacities: seven in the roundhouse, four on the rip track, two in the ice house and two in 'coal.' None had, as yet, filed papers for citizenship.

Enderlin's Diamond Jubilee book makes note of the Greeks who were present in the early decades: "Perhaps the most colorful figures of the early years were the Greek workers employed in the yards and on the road crews. Mostly young men, they differed from other immigrants in that few brought their families with them and apparantly they planned to make a stake and go back home. Unable to speak English, they relied on the foreman to handle their business affairs ... many lived in shacks near the roundhouse, and in the spring at the time of the Greek Orthodox Easter, a couple cars were shunted into the siding. Then the time was that the traditional Greek foods and wines were prepared and a several day feast and celebration took place."

A century ago one can easily see that a 'caste' system was present on every western railroad, whether Soo, the GN or the NP; old American employees were 'superior' to certain 'foreign types.' In fact, internal railroad communications, as found in company files,

Thrashing rig of John & Julie Baker 1910

An early American dream — the shear abundance of North Dakota wheat is exemplified in the threshing portrait from 1916 above — five grain wagons, eight bundle wagons, the separator, steam engine and waterwagon.

often classed southern and eastern European immigrants as 'foreign,' while British Isles' immigrants and some northern Europeans were 'white.' A note found in Soo files from 1913 has the special roadmaster saying, "white [i.e. English-speaking] labor only is employed in relaying; spikers and tongsmen receive 25 cents more a day than common labor. It has been proven beyond a doubt that it pays to organize this way."

The caste system was apparent in the 1910 Enderlin census: twenty four 'engineers' are listed, and of that number 22 were American-born, one was of Norwegian-birth and one was from England. Twenty seven 'conductors' are recorded; 23 were born in the U.S., two were from England and two were from Canada. Without question, British Isles' or long-time Americans were in privileged positions; 'hunkies' and 'dagos' were common laborers. So in spite of its rather sympathetic attitude towards 'foreigners' even the Soo Line had its limitations. Remember, too, that the Soo tracks like those of all western lines were dotted with frame company structures popularly (as well as in official company literature) called 'dago houses.'

Did any of the foreign-born laborers remain in the Dakotas? At least in the case of Enderlin, one long-time Greek farm family is still part of that city's rural community. This family is not alone in the state as Greeks took land elswhere, whether in Soo, NP or GN territory. A 1912 North Dakota news item reported, to our present day amazement, that at least 100 Greek men had left farmsteads to return to their homeland and fight in the Greek-Turkish war.

The movement of foreign individuals into this country did not always receive the blessings of the United States government. Not every nation was on the preferred list. The Chinese exclusion laws, dating back to the 1880s were in place. The hard fact is that Asians were not welcomed at the nation's points of entry; some students and merchants could come, but permanent Chinese immigrants were not accepted. It was here that the Soo Line entered the picture. Taking advantage of a more relaxed policy in Canada, hopeful Chinese, both before and after the turn of the century, would arrive at the nation's ports and subsequently seek to enter the country. Railroad corridors were the obvious way to do this. Portal, and to a lesser extent Pembina, were key entrances to the States. Entry through Washington and Montana meant railways which led back to the west coast cities. Portal, especially, allowed direct

Marketing grain in Kenmare circa 1900. Unusual in this scene is the mixed hitch. Note the ox on the left and the horse on right.

access to Minneapolis and Chicago via the Soo route diagonally across North Dakota. To prevent illegal Chinese incursions the U.S. government made Portal an immigration checkpoint. Repeatedly, in the 1890s and early 1900s, North Dakota newspapers reported the detention and deportation of individuals who sought to come into America's interior via the Soo Line. Pembina was a problem, but Portal was of particular significance. Accordingly, as early as 1894, an official Chinese Immigration Agent was posted in that Soo Line town and a Chinese detention house, complete with bars and locks was put into place.

The 'Chinese problem' was highlighted in a celebrated trial held in Fargo through the winter of 1899-1900. In this case the government sought to determine the legal status of 79 Chinese-born individuals. Forty-seven were eventually deported, two were dismissed and thirty were admitted to the United States.

As late as the 1920s, Portal was still a focus of Chinese 'problems.' Chinese whiskey was being sent into the States, bottled as 'soy' in fancy oriental-styled bottles. The deception was uncovered and such containers were duly destroyed in the city dump. The disposal job, however, was done with less than enthusiastic precision, for local residents salvaged some of the contents, strained it and used it for "personal use." It was deemed a "very good whiskey."

Assessing it all, one can say that the Soo Line, coming late to the Dakota prairies and steppes, was focused on agricultural haulage and its responsibility to the Canadian Pacific. Its mission was not to rearrange the social landscape in any large scale way.

However; along with the Great Northern, Northern Pacific and Milwaukee Road, it did help thousands of people acquire new land, new lives and for many, great opportunities. And...the Soo over its wide area of service proved to be a quiet and unspectacular conduit of good will and opportunity in opening a portion of the American Dream.

William Sherman
Associate Professor, Sociology
North Dakota State University

The Wheat Line

The 300 miles of Soo Line rails from Thief River Falls to Kenmare had its conception in 1902 as T. I. Hurd explored and evaluated this territory in conjunction with the proposed Winnipeg extension. The Winnipeg line was graded and built northward from Glenwood through western Minnesota during 1903-04. Planning the Wheat Line had gone on concurrently by Pennington and his staff at Minneapolis. Actual surveying did not start until 1905, however; the entire 300 miles were graded and rails were laid during that one season.

Pictorial coverage of this line has already been provided in *Part I* pp 44-51. An excellent presentation of the problems the Soo encountered with the Great Northern and Jim Hill can be found in John C. Hudson's "North Dakota's Railway War of 1905" (*North Dakota History Vol 48, No 1. 1981*).

Construction of the Wheat Line was financed by the Soo's issuance of 4% mortgage bonds which were guaranteed by the Canadian Pacific.

Immediately upon the announcment of construction efforts the campaign for settlers started. As can be seen in the photo on this page and others, it was not unusual to have five to eight grain elevators in business by 1912. Immigration and settlement efforts continued in full force until the eve of World War I. The following article from the *Portal International* in 1915 will illustrate the ongoing search for better opportunities:

FOURTEEN IMMIGRANT CARS ON WAY TO TOLLEY, N.D.

Fourteen carloads of immigrants' goods passed through Minot Friday, October 8 in a Soo Line fast freight destined for Tolley, North Dakota where they will locate on land. In the same train was an accommodation car in which the families of the immigrants were travelling. This car contains all conveniences for eating and sleeping as well as the preparation of food. The men in charge of the cars are thus enabled to 'eat at home' while making the trip. The settlers came from points in eastern Iowa and western Illinois and are substantial and well fixed farmers who are coming to North Dakota to make better homes and larger opportunities for themselves.

Two years ago the Soo Line began the work of immigration for this portion of the northwest and placed the matter in the hands of Major J.S. Murphy, formerly of Minot. He worked last year with more enthusiasm than results, but he never gave up on the plans that he was laying would in time yield the results both he and the railroad were hoping for. The road spent something like $20,000 last year in an effort to get settlers interested in lands along its lines in the state...

September 1905

Tolley, North Dakota had seven grain elevators in 1912. Here we see six of them with a 60 horsepower Case steamer pulling eight grain wagons to market. Wooden spoke wheels were standard.

Al Ohrt Collection

Landsford was served by both the former Great Northern line out of Granville as well as the Wheat Line. The old time farm days are important here with their annual steam threshers' reunion.

The rotary ties up at Russell not quite midway between Overly and Kenmare. January 1917.

Minneapolis - Mar.8,1943

TO ALL SECTION FOREMAN:

We recently had a serious personal injury case account a locomotive engineer struck on the head by a flexible grain spout attached to the permanent spout of a grain elevator on a house track.

We have recently called to the attention of all concerned the importance of maintaining full 8 feet clearance from the center of the track horizontally, measured to any obstructions such as elevator spouts, platforms or anything else that is placed inside the clearance. All agents have been instructed to watch this clearance situation closely. However we have a good many stations where there are no agents and will have to rely on section foreman and roadmasters to police this situation and call to the attention of the elevator men or building owners to the necessity of maintaining a proper clearance so that accidents such as above will not occur.

You will please consider this part of your duty, and effective at once you will make periodical checks and see that such a condition is not allowed to prevail.Talk to the building owners and advise them that State Law requires full 8' clearance and the lease under which they are permitted to occupy our property has a clause that requires this full legal clearance. Section men will promptly report any difficulty they may have in securing the cooperation of building owners to their roadmaster, who in turn will endeavor to persuade the building owner or lessee on our property to promptly remedy the clearance situation, and, if they fail to obtain any cooperation, the roadmaster will make a report to this office.

If you find any particularly dangerous situation, the dispatcher should be promptly notified to issue a bulletin so that trainmen can be properly warned and avoid accident until the situation is corrected.

cc: C.L. Simpson   T.Z. Krumm
      All Superintendents
      Roadmasters

Coal and Water Facilities- Wheat Line - 1943

Viking	Water tank 1.3 miles west
Warren	Water
Oslo	Coal and Water
Forest River	Water 0.7 miles west
Fordville	Coal, Water and Turntable
Adams	Coal and Water
Loma	Water 0.9 miles east
Egeland	Coal, Water and Wye
Armourdale	Wye
Bisbee	Water 1 mile east
Rolette	Water
Overly	Coal, Water and Turntable
Gardena	Water
Kramer	Water 4.6 miles west
Eckman	Coal
Greene	Water 1.1 miles east
Kenmare	Coal, Water and Turntable
Thief River Falls	Coal, Water and Turntable
Whitman	Water 2.08 miles west
Darby	Coal and Water
Comstock	Water
Fillmore	Water
Orris	Water
Drake	Coal, Water and Wye

John Shoenig on the platform with two trainmen at Grano circa 1915. This same Schoenig was in partnership with a Mr. Bridwell in the hardware business in Grano. It was not unusual for depot agents or section crew to have interests in local business ventures.

Lansford Historical Society

Below is what was left of Lawrence's last run, "I had her going 20 [mph] or so and I never even felt the air go out—anyway, it was more than a @#%$* pileup and as I had 40 years in with the Soo, I just walked away and never took a run again." Extra west October 1985 at Tolley, North Dakota.

Lawrence Drabus Collection

Grano, like almost all of the Wheat Line villages, had its birth in 1905. It reached a peak population of 112 in 1920.

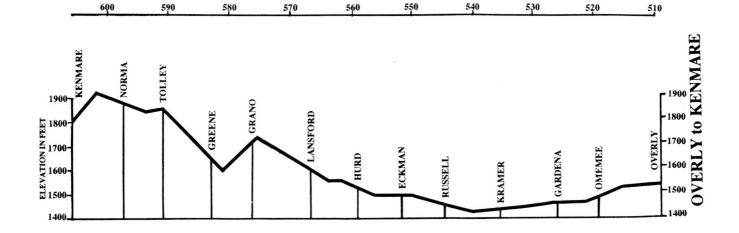

Gordon Twedt Collection

Fairdale in 1913. The first station west of Adams in the Park River Valley is aptly named. Notice the fading two-tone paint job on the Soo Standard second class depot.

Millard Nelson Collection

Above: Consol **426** balances on the Fordville turntable with its snow plow still attached, even though the green grass would indicate a summer time photo. The Fordville Turntable was an 'air kick' type with the air pressure coming from the engine's air line.

Charles W. Bohi

How many games at this field have been interrupted by the passage of a train? This view at Lankin, N.D. looks west and **4401** and **4598** are working the elevators.

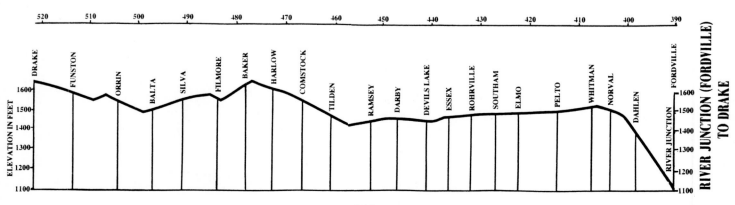

Fordville

The three photos to the left and above show the sequence of bringing a Mikado out from the Fordville roundhouse, taking on water and being turned on the turntable. (circa 1948)

All Photos: Wallace Pfeiffer

Below: **3005** a heavy Mikado built by Dunkirk in 1920. These Wisconsin Central Class L-20 engines were identical to Soo Line class L-3. Weight was 149 tons with 63" drivers. These were the heavy haul freight engines for the Soo on many secondary routes.

Wallace Pfeiffer

Stuart Nelson

Even in 1957 engines were turned on the Fordville table. This Baldwin DRS 4-4-15 1500 horsepower diesel just came off service from the west on train No. 212. The Soo had eight of these Baldwin road switchers (built in 1947-48). Many were used on North Dakota's branch lines.

1947 view of Egeland depot with tank, windmill and coal dock in distance. The name Egeland came as a reward to Axel Egeland - a banker at Bisbee - because of his efforts in securing right of way for a portion of the Soo's Wheat Line.

William Egan

*Soo Standard **19*** *arrives* at Kramer in 1907. Note the buckboard on the left in front and at least four elevators on the left. Although there are lace curtains in the upstairs living quarters of the Standard second class depot, not a woman is in sight.

Ed. Wertheim Collection

January snow and cold in 1958 as mixed train No. 217 heads north from Egeland to Armourdale. This short branch (now abandoned) is the sole instance in which the Soo parallels the Great Northern branch along the Wheat Line.

Stuart Nelson

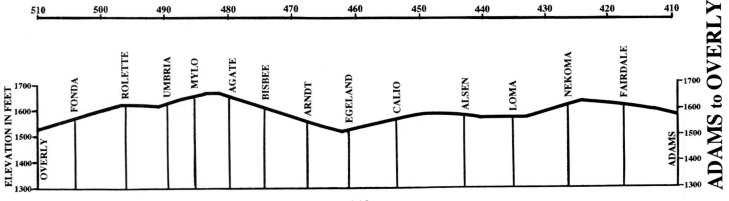

ADAMS to OVERLY

This is the engine Harry is firi

Adams was initially named Sarles (at that time Governor of North Dakota) by Soo Line officials, but quickly changed when it was learned that there was another North Dakota village with the same name. Actually, Jim Hill named a GN town to honor the Governor, and he carried more weight in N.D. than the Soo. This 1907 view shows the engineer and his fireman 'Harry' standing next to their D-2 **143.**

Pete Bonesteel Collection

John Gjevre

Further east along the Wheat Line we find one of several joint GN/Soo depots. This one at Ardoch near the Red River is of GN design and ownership—not a 'union depot.' (Summer 1970)

Baldwin 1500 hp Demo at Overly, 1946

The Soo bought from all the early diesel manufacturers and although the first road switchers were Alco products, by the early 60's it was apparent that the Soo was to be an all GM-EMD powered railroad. Only the 10-800 series GE U Boats were to crack the EMD buying habit.

Stuart Nelson Collection

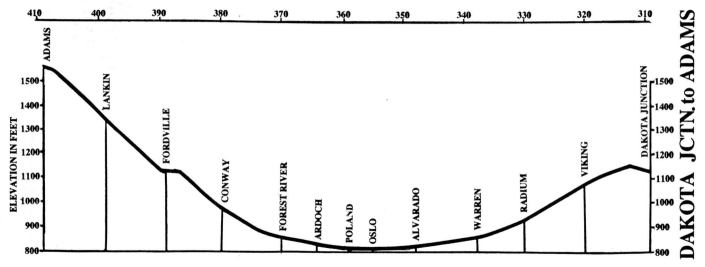

Today there is a vanishing minority that actually lived in Soo Line depots, either as agents or as part of an agent's family. We are indebted to Carol Monroe, wife of a long time Soo agent on the Wheat Line, for her contribution. This brings a much needed woman's perspective to the overall history of the Soo, as well as other railroads in the Upper Midwest. Although this is a personal history, it brings each of us closer to those happy and difficult times.

Stormy winter nights in North Dakota may seem to offer few compensations, but my husband and I actually cherished such nights during the years we lived at the depot. When the time came for the early morning train from Oslo, Jim had only to walk down the stairway to work. Standing by the upstairs window, I would watch with him until the train lights emerged from the snow.

The Soo Line Depot became our first home in 1956. Over the years it served many people in the railroad community, creating a home at times for them as well. The depot was a shelter in the time of storm for travellers, railmen, and neighbors, many of whom shared lasting friendships with us. Our waiting room downstairs was always open to snow-bound travelers, and the men from the American Crystal Sugar factory going to or from East Grand Forks would often times be our overnight guests. Our waiting room also served as a makeshift cafeteria for stranded men during the big flood. I would cook for them in the little kitchen Jim and I had fixed up together. To me, the house was the most beautiful and welcoming place in the world. After moving in, we immediately set about making the rooms cozy, putting in running water, a bathroom, kitchen cupboards, and yes, even a washer and dryer. Turquoise and pink were the 'in' colors in those days, and so turquoise blue was the color of my new davenport and chair. The depot only had one bedroom, but it didn't seem small for the five of us. Somehow we found room for a double bed, roll-away bed, crib, stove and two chests of drawers.

Bigger is not necessarily better, and the result of 'improvements' and expansion for the railroad has often been the loss of personal connections. To me, personal relations with the people who travel and work on the rails has always been the most important part of the Soo Line Depot. Relationships are the true connections that hold the branches of the railroad together.

In those early years at the depot our lives were shaped by the connections we formed with many groups of travellers and railroad men. Elevator men, relief workers, and bridge gangs all made unique contributions to the railroad community. Bridge gangs would arrive and move in their equipment, train cars, and even a couple of trailer houses. The area became their neighborhood, and we became their friends. And our section men, especially, were like our

family. Each day was a different conversation; and of course, we brought coffee and goodies downstairs for them again and again. The elevator men, too, were special. Whenever they brought a billing over we would all share in coffee or sometimes just a chat about local issues or new developments on the line.

As time went on, the railroad community came to share in more than simply coffee and goodies at the depot. Birthdays, holidays, and significant family events also served to connect us together. When our children celebrated their birthdays in February and November we not only invited neighbor children to the parties but whole families as well. I'll never forget a particular birthday 'party' which some of our friends shared.

It was a blizzarding winter evening and I had just made up a hotdish for some unexpected overnight guests. I was expecting my third child at the time and was humorously joking and telling them that I might just go into the hospital in the storm—Well, lo and behold, I did! As I went into labor, the storm intensified and we all began to worry about the prospect of making it to the hospital. The wind was raging violently outside, shaking the windows and blowing snow under the door of the waiting room. But we decided to try to make it to town. So, with the sturdy snowplow starting first and three of our guests going with my husband to shovel our way out, we headed that night for the hospital in Warren—ten miles away. The section man's wife—a generous, good-hearted woman—stayed with our two young children because the storm left our original intended baby sitter stranded at Frazee, MN.

We made it somehow to Warren and I told my husband to leave me off at the hospital and go right home and attend to things there. I admitted myself to the hospital and immediately felt calmer, knowing I was safe with the doctor there. The doctor was relieved to see me. He had earlier tried to call me and tell me what to do if the baby should come early, but the telephone lines had gone down in the storm. The baby arrived the next day, and the storm calmed, leaving an abundance of soft, white snow.

The storms up in Warren often last well into the so-called spring, making Easter celebrations a frosty prospect for travellers and railmen. Each year at Easter, we would have an overnight guest staying in our waiting room. One year I remember we were getting ready for services and noticed a body curled up by the big coal stove. It was a cold, exhausted young man. I told him we were on our way to church and would be back home for dinner. We urged him to stay for the Easter dinner, but he hesitated, so I packed him a lunch, milk and gloves to keep his hands warm. We went on to church and left our guest to spend his Easter Sunday in the waiting room, warming his hands by the large coal-blackened stove.

Seeing holidays spent in this way, my husband would always reflect on his very first job on the railroad, many years before. Jim had been very young and scared to death of going off by himself. Having no car, he had to take his bedroll and personal things on the train—carrying his pack about with him like a hobo. He'd be away from family and friends for many days and months at a time, not even getting home for holidays. But a holiday spent alone in a railway depot is not the greatest loneliness a person can know. I remember on Christmas Eve taking a telegram to some neighbors in the country. There had been a death in their family. Before we drove

Stuart Nelson Collection

The Oslo depot in 1915. Forty-nine years before the fire incident described agent T.A. Suprey and caretaker Leslie Wygant pose. T.A. Suprey was the grandfather of Leslie Suprey, author of *Steam Trains of the Soo.*

the forty miles to my family's house for Christmas Eve we loaded the car with kids, presents, and food, heading first to the neighbors to deliver that telegram.

I'm glad our two older children had the opportunity to grow up in the depot, surrounded by the kindness of travellers and trainmen. Our youngest child didn't have the privilege of growing up in the depot and missed out on some of the childhood joys (and mishaps) our life there provided.

Our children, when they were young, didn't have a lot of mechanical toys—or toys at all. Even so, their friends who did have toys preferred playing at the depot where they always had a lot of paper boxes to play in along with a basketball hoop and net my husband had set up. The boys loved to dribble and shoot basketball and the depot practice eventually payed off for our middle son, who became a key player on the Warren Ponies basketball team. The boys also learned to play baseball, getting regular noontime lessons one summer from a bat-swinging young relief agent who came to work at the depot during Jim's vacation. The people who found their way to the depot almost invariably took an interest

in my boys, teaching them games and skills, and instilling in them a respect for the railroad.

My sons did learn to respect the rail and trains very much and they taught their friends to do the same. They saw the force and majesty of the railroad and recognized that even though the depot might afford opportunites for play, trains were powerful machines that required caution—and work. I remember on winter afternoon watching the section men getting into a coal car and showing the boys how to help unload it. My sons were right there in their snowpants, jackets and scarves and mittens, helping out. They were diligent and careful, and managed each to make a quarter for their efforts.

I sometimes worried about my children as they played at the depot. The depot, as I mentioned, was always a shelter to travellers and linemen, and we did our best to be hospitable and make them at home. But sometimes we found ourselves unwilling hosts to strangers whom we feared to trust.

One one occasion, I received a call from my closest neighbor, Donna Monk, saying an escaped convict was running loose in [Alvarado] and had been spotted in the neighborhood. He was known to be very dangerous. Her husband worked for the city and was alerted to the escape as well and was helping to look for him. Donna and I were on the phone until the wee hours of the morning and later heard that the criminal had been in our garage and had been lurking about the yard at the depot. We were terribly afraid and jumpy for a long time after that, even when the danger was past.

Another time, we left the children in the care of an older lady while we were attending a wedding in town. It was a cool Saturday afternoon, and they were playing hide and seek—jumping in and out of old boxes and hiding behind the sheds. They went to look in the open door of a rail car and came upon a tramp napping on the bed of burlap sacks. He was dirty and unshaven and stared fiercely at them. The baby-sitter grabbed the children and ran up into the house, locking the upstairs door. When Jim and I came home, the children were unperturbed, but the neighbor lady was shaken. Children don't always realize that they are in danger, but a parent never forgets such things.

Another thing I'll never forget is the fire that struck the depot and its terrifying aftermath. We had been away for part of the summer at the family farm 20 miles east of Alvarado. We'd suffered horribly from the heat in the steaming upstairs rooms at the depot so we pitched camp at the old house for those few months. The farm was a restful change of scene for the children and for us adults. Unfortunately, things did not remain restful for very long. I remember it was about 1:00 AM when we were awakened by Knut Torgerson (one of the section men) telling us the elevator was burning down. What a terror! We hurried to the depot to take out things from the house that were keepsakes. The heat upstairs was so intense we choked and coud barely breathe. Nearby, the elevator was being consumed by tall, spiralling flames. We grabbed pictures and a few personal things and fled. The elevator burned completely down, so they had to go about building a new one. I'm thankful, however, that they kept the depot and other buildings pretty wet and managed to save them from destruction.

Ron Olin Collection

Olso, Warren and Radium in northwest Minnesota are all part of Marshall county, with Warren being the county seat. Jim Hill's Saint Paul and Pacific reached here during a frenzy of building in 1878 as this predecessor of the Great Northern stretched from Crookston to Winnipeg. In 1905, as the Soo went west with the Wheat Line, Warren became a two-railroad town. Postcard view, circa 1912.

What happened after the fire was, for me as a parent, even more terrifying than the fire. It didn't take any time before construction began to replace the burned elevator. When the workers finished the building, they didn't immediately enclose the 80' outdoor ladder. Standing exposed and inviting, that ladder was an irresistable lure to our five year old boy. He was an outstanding climber and decided to head for the top of the elevator. And so it was that I happened to look out my upstairs window one day and saw a group of people looking up. I followed their gaze and saw to my horror MY SON—eighty feet in the air. I realized my hair was going to turn gray in an instant if I didn't do something FAST. I ran outside, and trying to stay calm, told him to come down exactly the way he had gone up. I held my breath as I watched him inching his way down the 80' ladder. When he finally came down I had a good lecture prepared (you can imagine the style and content), but was so deliriously happy to see he was okay all I could do was hold him. I forgot all about the speech. The protective enclosure went up the next day and there were no climbing terrors thereafter.

After the elevator burned we became very cautious about fires. Many nights when it was 40 below with a tough wind battering the dry old yellow building, we wouldn't sleep much thinking about the possibility of fire in the depot. We always planned our fire escape routes with the kids. I'm not sure how we would have made it out the window in case of a winter fire, considering that our windows were always draped with several layers of blankets and coverings to keep out the wind and the cold. We would wake often on windy nights, and watch the stove with Argus eyes.

Our younger boy is also gone—killed by a car when he was only nine years old. The world changes so disorientingly. When I think about the years my family spent living beside the tracks, I am still so grateful for the warm community that surrounded us and the memories we have. I will never forget the picnics I enjoyed with my children under the railroad bridge each spring. I will not forget the kindness of people who were 'just passing through.' Although our place is gone now, my husband and I were ourselves not really passing through but rather making a commitment. Jim worked for the Soo Line for 42 years. Until his first surgery, he never missed a day of work. That's a lot of time for a man to spend with one company, a long time to dedicate to a single evolving community. And I feel I've spent a long time on the Soo Line as well, watching out my upstairs window for the train lights breaking through the snow.

Otto Dobnick

Elevators in small communities have to be resourceful when switching and moving grain cars—especially unit train loading of 25 or 52 card. Here a John Deere 'yard switcher' does the honors at Radium, MN on the Wheat Line (6-27-88). Since leaving the Soo, the Monroe's have made their home farming south of Radium. The discovery of radium by the Curies in 1898 was still newsworthy during 1905 when the Wheat Line was pushed through.

Drake

To the right and below one can observe the tragic Drake wreck of November 6, 1912. Class D-1 Mogul **202** was at the head of the passenger train. The wrecker is sending the Wisconsin Central caboose to recycling and oblivion.

Both photos by Redding: Gordon Twedt Collection

As these photos depict, Drake was a minor but busy hub on the Soo's main line through North Dakota. In 1909 a branch was built west from Drake to Max and on to the Missouri river at Sanish to help tap the Fort Berthold Indian reservation which opened at that time.

Then in 1912, seeing a need for a short cut to Duluth and eastern markets via the Great Lakes, 132 miles were constructed from Drake connecting with the Wheat Line at Fordville.

Below: Unloading rails for the new yard in Drake during June of 1912.

Photo by Redding: Gordon Twedt Collection

151

Eastbound local freight spring 1949.

Gerald Wodarz

Left: The Drake yard enginehouse windmill and tank in 1957. Note the ancient tank car set on piers for diesel fuel storage.

Stuart Nelson

Below: **774**, **741**, and **776** eastbound at Drake on train No. 940 May 22. 1984. This manifest is from the CP at Portal destined for Minneapolis.

Bob Wise

Devils Lake

Stuart Nelson

Mixed train No. 216 eastbound at Devils Lake. This standard first class depot was faced with brick veneer and still stands in 1994. Running time for the 132 miles from Drake to Fordville was seven hours.

Once every praire town had a depot. On the Soo LIne, most of the classic two-story 'Second Class' stations still remained in the late 1960's. In 1992, however, the only depot **4421** will pass is this one at Devils Lake, N.D. A brick version of its more ornate 'First Class' depot, the Devils Lake station, was typical of those built by the Soo Line in communities of greater importance.

July 8, 1992   **Charles W. Bohi**

Right: Almost hotter than Hades in Devils Lake on July 1, 1970; a Soo brakeman flexes his muscles.

John Gjevre

153

The big 'city' of Harlow in the late seventies. Founded in 1912, it had a peak population of 100. At the time that this photo was taken, there was a a grocery store, pool hall, garage, and a post office. Today about all that remains besides the homes and church are the grain elevators which move grain on the Soo in 52 car units.

Magnus Lysne Collection

In 1981, the Soo installed its first solar powered signal installation near Dahlen, ND. Panels, seen at the left, convert sunlight directly to D.C. electric current to power the signals and recharge batteries, allowing the crossing gates to operate at night as well as during cloudy weather. Solar power is used for such purposes when conventional electric service is unavailable.

Soo Line Railroad

The Plummer Line
with additional photo coverage of the Brooten line.

The Plummer Line was constructed in 1909-10 in order to provide direct access for North Dakota and Montana wheat to Duluth and the Great Lakes inland waterway. It more or less paralleled the Great Northern's Grand Forks-Duluth mainline and thus it is no surprise that much of the line has been abandoned in favor of trackage rights over the present day Burlington Northern. In 1956 the short segment Bemidji-Schley was taken up and the portion from Schley to Moose Lake was pulled in 1985. Much of the logging and pulpwood movements of the Soo in Minnesota were on this line although logging was important for a brief time along the Brooten-Moose Lake line as well.

Perhaps a brief imaginary tour along the original Plummer Line will help bring to life this important connecting segment in Soo Line history. Plummer, at first just a farming stop along the Winnipeg line, was first settled by Charles Plummer in 1881 when his mill was built on the Clearwater river nearby. The railroad had a well and water tank here. Ten miles east is Oklee, famed for Coya Knutson (Minnesota 9th District Congresswoman 1955-1959) whose husband ran a one person recall with his 'come back Coya' campaign. She lost the re-election but he didn't win either in that she divorced him. Twelve miles further east the Soo crosses a deep gully which is along the highest beach ridge of ancient Lake Agassiz. Obviously, this town just had to be called plain GULLY.

Tracks through Gonvick, Clearbrook, and Leonard took the Soo through deep forest country until

John Gjevre Collection

Richard Anderson on patrol at Gonvick in 1916.

Richard Anderson

Right: D-2 Mogul **150** heads a short way freight into Gonvick during early spring 1916. Note the low snowplow attached to the wooden pilot and the two little stock cars behind the first car.

Richard Anderson

Pinewood

The train comes to this forest community from the west. Note the pulpwood car on the siding with the loading dock for the stockyards just beyond.
Note also the Soo Standard unisex outhouse on the right. (1948)

Tom Millar

The Plummer Line was constructed in 1909-10 in order to provide direct access for North Dakota and Montana wheat to Duluth and the Great Lakes inland waterway. It more or less paralleled the Great Northern's Grand Forks-Duluth mainline and thus it is no surprise that much of the line has been abandoned in favor of trackage rights over the present day Burlington Northern. In 1956 the short segment Bemidji-Schley was taken up and the portion from Schley to Moose Lake was pulled in 1985. Much of the logging and pulpwood movements of the Soo in Minnesota were on this line although logging was important for a brief time along the Brooten-Moose Lake line as well.

Perhaps a brief imaginary tour along the original Plummer Line will help bring to life this important connecting segment in Soo Line history. Plummer, at first just a farming stop along the Winnipeg line, was first settled by Charles Plummer in 1881 when his mill was built on the Clearwater river nearby. The railroad had a well and water tank here. Ten miles east is Oklee, famed for Coya Knutson (Minnesota 9th District

Bemidji's Union depot for the Minnesota and International was completed in 1911 by Baily and Marsh of Minneapolis for about $20,000. The first Soo Line train to use the new depot was No. 162 from Thief River Falls to Duluth on July 27, 1911. The depot has a red brick exterior and grey marble and oak offer a most handsome interior. This was one of the few early depots to use steam heat. Bemidji is a Chippewa word meaning 'Lake with river flowing through.' The actress Jane Russell was born here.

State Historical Society of Wisconsin

Bemidji

Union Station from the north in thie 1920 postcard view. The Minnesota and International (an NP subsidiary) built the depot and the Soo used it until the end of passenger service. The Great Northern refused to use the facility and had its own depot in downtown Bemidji about a block away. To the left is the main waiting room and on the right is the women's waiting room and baggage room. The Minnesota and International was absorbed into the Northern Pacific about 1940.

1920   Pete Bonesteel Collection

Lloyd Berger

W.M. Flint

Above Left: The Bemidji freighthouse aged well and gracefully as depicted in this 1964 portrait by Lloyd Berger.

Above Right: But one carload of pulpwood behind GP7 **377** in this September 1973 photo (the freight house was still in use at this time). Eastbound way freight.

Left: Bemidji freighthouse interior circa 1915. Left to right: Charles Paul, Arnold Bakkum, unknown, George Knight, George Armstrong.

Beltrami County Historical Society

Federal Dam

Above: Coach track is clear but rip track is full in 1912-1915 Federal Dam Roundhouse. Lead has ashpit, water tank, sand house, coal shed, and ice house facilities.

Left: Eight stall roundhouse, boilerhouse, oilhouse and rip track storehouses of 1912-1915 Federal Dam indicate the extent of hopes of traffic volume on the Plummer Line that never really materialized.

Below: the rear of Federal Dam's roundhouse. Note the wood sheathed siding.

Because of its proximity to Minnesota Highway 200, the Remer depot has been immortalized on multiple occasions with a Kodak. Here it stands without any trees in 1920.

Bemidji during 1901-03 towards International Falls. The Northern Pacific controlled the Minnesota International as it reached International Falls in 1907 and purchased it outright in 1941. Soo Line rails reached Bemidji in 1910 as the Plummer Line was completed from Plummer to Federal Dam.

Also near Bemidji is Itasca State Park, the true headwaters of the Mississippi River. To the north one can find the renowned International Language Villages of Concordia College with summer language (Norwegian, German, French, Swedish, and Finnish) camps surrounding Turtle River Lake.

First stop east of Bemidji was Scribner, just a water stop in steam days. Going on southeast and always south of the Mississippi, the tracks reached Federal Dam. Here there was a division point with roundhouse, shops, coal, water and yards, built by a youthful and exuberant Soo during construction years 1910 and on. It never fulfilled the planned expectations and in 1990 the census counted just 118 residents and still shrinking. A great deal of white

Below: Soo Standard 4-4-0 **28** with Eastward Thief River Falls to Duluth local. At Remer, October 27, 1914.

Left: No. 65 with Baldwin engine 353 stops at Remer per timetable notation "for meals." August 8, 1955.

Douglas Wick Collection

Along the Brooten line on Mille Lacs Lake circa 1914: For a brief time, the Soo received lumber and transshipped supplies to lumber camps and resorts on the lake.

and Norway pine had been harvested in this area around the turn of the century, but the lakes, bogs and simply inadequate soil never made for a farmer's paradise.

Twenty miles south and east from Federal Dam is Remer, one of the very few small towns along this line viable today with a 1990 census of 342- thanks to tourist business from the nearby lakes and its location on Minnesota 200. Remer's second class depot proudly stands where it always stood – nicely along the empty grade which is now a snowmobile trail. Nearby, Weyerhauser had a logging operation that went north into the woods some 15 miles with its Shay locomotives. Frank King's map of Minnesota

To the right: Section crew at Swatara March 15, 1917. This photo of 'safety last' motorcar #213 was taken by Richard Anderson, 99 yrs young in 1995. Anderson hired out in 1914, and after a stint with the army railroad service in France, he worked for the Soo as section foreman for nearly fifty years.

Moose Lake, MN was the junction point for the 'Brooten Line' with the 'Plummer Line.'

Wayne Olsen

160

logging railroads shows a Pine Tree Lumber Company that had been active in this area. In addition, south of the tracks, Fred Blair also logged all the way from near Remer to Swatera.

Deeper into the forest through Aitkin County the rails reached minihamlets such as Swatera and Pallisade. Here the tracks crossed the Mississippi before climbing to McGregor. In 1929 McGregor became the junction point for the Cuyuna Range line to Crosby-Ironton and Riverton. A diamond took Soo Line tracks across the Northern Pacific's Brainerd-Duluth line. Lawler had been the original junction for Soo Line rails going to the Cuyuna Range towns of Crosby and Riverton. The historic ore pooling agreement between the NP and Soo allowed the Soo to use the Northern Pacific line into the Cuyuna as well as the latter's ore dock in Superior. Incidentally, the Savanna Portage, which provided fur traders in the eighteenth and early nineteenth centuries with a route for canoe traffic between the Mississippi and Lake Superior is nearby. A state park has facilities and an interpretive center nearby for those who wish to appreciate it.

The tiny hamlets of Automba and Kettle River provided little lading following World War II and thus it is not surprising that so little fanfare or opposition came to the Soo's plans for abandonment in 1985.

On to Moose Lake (1990 population: 1206) where the Plummer tracks joined the line from Brooten; it is but 51 miles to the 'Zenith City'–Duluth–at the head of the navigation on Lake Superior.

Stuart Nelson Collection

In 1929 the McGregor depot was moved to the NP/Soo crossing diamond. This photo shows the newly moved depot resting on cribbing made of ties.

Richard Anderson Photo

Above Right: Brick tower owned by the Soo at McGregor for the protection of the NP Brainerd to Duluth main. March 1915.

Interior of the McGregor crossing tower. (March 1915). This tower became redundant in 1929 as the Northern Pacific and Soo agreed to use NP tracks as part of the pool agreement.

Richard Anderson

126 –a D2 Mogul is typical of the lighter motive power used on both the Plummer and Brooten lines. The rescue engine mentioned below was likely similar. Above photo taken on the Brooten line about 1913.

The great Moose Lake fire during October 1918 consumed 2,000 square miles and affected some 6,000 additional square miles in the forested area near and about the Cuyuna Iron Range. In all 525 died and perhaps as many as 8,000 families were homeless. In the immediate vicinity of Moose Lake 453 lives were lost and there a 28 foot tall granite monument stands today to commemorate this tragedy.

Soo Line towns along both the Plummer and the Brooten Lines were affected including Remer, Shovel Lake, Swatara, Palisade McGregor, East Lake Lawler, Aitkin, Automba and Kettle River as well as Moose Lake itself. Communication was impossible as the fire scorched and burned telegraph lines and many railroad bridges were also consumed. After word of the

conflagration reached Minneapolis a special train was dispatched to the burning towns to evacuate the homeless. Many Soo Line families that worked Cuyuna Range jobs lived in Lawler at the time and a mercy train with all the men, women and children left only moments before the flames consumed the Lawler depot and it exploded from the heat.

Mercifully cool weather and rain came to quench the fire only to have the homeless miserable in the damp October days. Many of the survivors thus weakened succumbed shortly to the devestating flu of 1918.

Even though the magnificient stands of white pine that attracted lumber men to this area are long gone, the Soo continued to haul pulpwood in cars such as these to the right. This accounted for much of the originating traffic on the Plummer Line.

Patrick Dorin

Stuart Nelson

No. 160 with Alco road freight **209B** *at Onamia, August 13, 1957.* The roundhouse is now gone and crews work from Glenwood to Superior (See also pages 52 and 53, *Part I*).

Right: Holdingford on the Brooten Line is in the midst of rich dairy country. August 9, 1973

Stuart Nelson

Left: Construction action at McGrath, MN in 1909. Wooden water towers were 'coopered' much like wooden barrels.

Soo Line Railroad Collection

This aerial view of the Cuyuna Range was taken in 1947. The Yawker's Mine is the upper left, the Immanuel the upper right, and the Portmouth the left center with the shaft for the Thompson in the lower right. The old main line to Riverton is also visible in the lower right. The main line east to Cuyuna and Moose Lake goes off to the upper left.

Much swampy country was encountered before the Soo could reach the Cuyuna. This narrow gauge tank engine is gingerly pushing dumpcars with fill on to a spidery trestle.

Gene Foote Collection

164

The Cuyana Range Ore Lines
by Patrick C. Dorin

Introduction

The Soo's heaviest trains carried the iron ore between the Cuyuna Iron Range and Superior, Wisconsin. The Cuyuna range is one of five iron ranges in the state of Minnesota. Although the Mesabi, the largest and most famous range, continues with its open pit mining in 1994, the Vermillion range near Ely and the Cuyuna range near Crosby have ceased all mining operations.

The Spring Valley range in southeastern Minnesota has long ceased shipments over the Chicago Great Western Railway and the Gunflint range in far northeastern Minnesota was never commercially viable.

Cuyuna ore shipments began at the Kennedy Mine in 1911. At that time the Soo Line provided the only rail access to the ore. A detailed history of this operation has been serialized in *The SOO* (the quarterly journal published by the Soo Line Historical and Technical Society). The Soo's Cuyuna Range operations were unique because of the ore traffic pooling agreement with the Northern Pacific.

The ore in the Cuyuna range lies in vertical planes or lenses and therefore early mining was all underground (as per the Kennedy mine). Rock in the Cuyuna is hard (due to the high manganese content), unlike the ore one finds in the Mesabi Range which is comparatively soft.

This chapter provides a brief history of mining, pool operations and train movements from mines to ore docks along with a pictorial review of the operations, mines and equipment.

Historical Sketch

Iron ore was discovered on the Cuyuna Range in 1903. This area is about 100 miles west of Duluth. Soo operations began April 11, 1911 as the first train of 42 cars was loaded at the Kennedy Mine. That day it traveled three miles east to Iron Hub where it was held until May 4th. Traveling towards Superior that day, a hopper door on one of the ore cars opened between Blackhoof and Frogner. This caused sixteen cars to derail. The remaining twenty six cars made it to Superior on May 5th. Ore from this tardy first shipment dropped into the steamboat *Alva* from the newly constructed Soo timber ore dock on May 27th; Cuyuna range ore thus became part of the nation's industrial heritage.

The Crosby-Ironton branch of the Soo Line had been built in 1910, the same year that the Plummer-Moose Lake Line was completed. Even though the Northern Pacific main had been built through the range years earlier, the Soo was the first to serve the iron mines. During 1913, the NP laid tracks into the mining area and completed work on their concrete ore dock in Superior.

During the late 1920's the NP and Soo began exploring possibilities of creating a joint operation and pooling agreement. By then the Soo's timber ore dock

View of the Kennedy Mine showing ore cars (80200 to 80499) in their original configuration and lettering scheme. The tailing pile is still rather small - the photo likely dates from 1912-1913.

Pete Bonesteel Collection

'Two horse power' wooden dump car being loaded by a steam shovel on a (narrow) eighteen inch gauge contractor's railway. The bog and mire were so treacherous that standard gauge construction methods were unthinkable.

Gene Foote Collection

The *Cuyuna Iron Range RR was* a small line built during 1909 to the NP at Aitkin. The NP was adamant about the freight rate for Cuyuna Range ore to the Twin Ports. Cuyler Adams, the mining engineer who discovered the range, felt otherwise and secretly joined with the Soo to build east to connect with the Soo's new Plummer - Moose Lake extension. This was done to the utter dismay of the Northern Pacific.

Gene Foote Collection

was in dire need of heavy rebuilding. After working out many individual problems, the two railroads signed an agreement not only to pool ore tonnage between the Cuyuna Range and Superior, but also to provide for the common use of facilities and equipment between Superior and Ironton. The pool agreement allowed the Soo to abandon its branch between Lawler and the range, as well as their classification yard and ore dock at Billings Park in Superior. Starting in 1929, the Soo operated over Northern Pacific tracks between McGregor and Ironton, as well as the NP facilities in Superior. With the BN merger in 1970, Soo ore trains operated in and out of the former Great Northern Allouez yard in Superior.

The last Soo train to haul Cuyuna ore came from the Virginia Mine during the fall of 1984. Since there are still manganese deposits on the Cuyuna, certain economic conditions could spark new life into this mining area. Soo Line tracks, however, are now gone and we have only memories of the ore trains of the Soo.

Soo Line ore operations can be divided into three interrelated categories: *mine runs and transfers, road haul, and finally, ore yard and dock operations.*

Second Unit 2407, a 1750 horsepower EMD GP9 flexes its muscles with the ore tonnage; Fall 1964. Note the heavy ballast indicative of the ongoing high quality maintenance so very necessary for these most heavy trains.

Soo Line Railroad

Mine Runs and Transfers

In early days, class D-2 Moguls were used on the mine runs and transfers. The job of the crew was to spot empties, pick up loads, and assemble trains for subsequent road-haul at the Iron Hub yards. A bit later, class F 2-8-0 locomotives were used for this complex and spread out duty. The Iron Hub yard remained in operation until the ore pooling agreement became effective for the 1929 season. Thereafter, the assignments operated out of the Northern Pacific yard between Ironton and Deerwood.

Since the pool agreement specified that switching hours were to be split between the two roads, each railroad provided an equal number of locomotives and crews. In the diesel era, Soo and NP motive power were often multiple-united for mining operations. The only Soo locomotives not M-U'd together were the Baldwin road switchers used during the 1950's.

The range crews did minimal classification work for the outbound ore trains. As the ore traffic declined during the 1960's and later, there were to be rather few such crew assignments. During that time, an extra would be sent to Ironton and that crew would switch the mines and assemble their own train.

All of the ore pulled from the mines was 'tagged' as to type - including the chemical content and whether it was crushed, lump or fines. This information was critical for the purpose of assembling ore boat cargos and appropriate dumping in the ore docks. During the times when dozens of mines were operating, assembling for dumping was an extremely complex operation.

By 1980, when only one mine remained in operation, the road crew would leave their caboose at Deerwood on the Burlington Northern, and run through Ironton en-route to the mine. At Trommald, ore cars were shoved into the mine and the crew would return to town and tie up for rest. After the mandatory off

A 2-6-0 assigned to switching service had the distinction of handling the first movement of ore out of the Kennedy Mine in the spring of 1911.

Wayne Olsen Collection

time, the train would travel light back to the mine. It would then bring the ore cars to Ironton and Deerwood where the caboose was added, thereafter taking the main to Superior.

Major League Railroading in Soo Line Land

Think of those days when 2-8-2's were handling 125 cars with synchronized chugging over the romantic clickity-clack — a veritable symphony in steel. After the advent of diesels, trains of up to 220 ore cars were handled out of the Cuyuna to and from Superior before the rapid decline in traffic during the mid sixties.

Prior to 1929, the Soo crews would run from the 21st street roundhouse in Superior to the Soo's own ore yard — entirely over Soo Line rails. All of this was changed by the ore pooling agreement. Soo trains operated to and from the Northern Pacific's Hill avenue ore yard in Superior as well as over the NP between McGregor and Ironton.

Since the ore traffic was split on a 50/50 basis, the two companies also split use of their ore cars based on capacity. Soo and NP cars were completely mixed together making for a most interesting appearing ore train.

Dieselization came in the form of pairs of EMD F units or Alco FA-1 road freight units at the beginning, with GP-9's cut in between. These road freight units were often part of a diesel pool that handled Twin City freights and between runs in Superior the locomotives would make a run out to the

The Riverton Livery barn housed the horses that worked on the mining projects, as well as for necessary taxi services.

Gene Foote Collection

167

range and back. With two road units the trains were about 125 cars long. Splicing in a geep would expand the consist to 150 cars. Still later, when the GP-30's were available, 220 ore cars were sometimes in the same consist.

The Burlington Northern merger changed some of the operating procedures. Although the pooling agreement remained in place, the Hill Avenue yard and NP dock in Superior closed. Soo trains began operating to and from the former Great Northern Allouez yard and docks in Superior. Finally, when the Allouez began only handling taconite pellets, all raw ore traffic interchanged with the Duluth, Missabe and Iron Range ore facility in Duluth. By this time, many of the Soo Line ore cars had been reassigned to rock and ballast service, and thus many DM&IR cars were seen on Soo Line ore service.

Ore Dock and Yard Operations

There were two eras of yard operations, *1911-1928 and 1929-1984.*

Yard operations had involved and complex switching orders since each boat load required an individual set of specifications. Shipments from several mines were blended in a process which had to take into consideration the physical characteristics of the ore; i.e. lump ore and fines, as well as the chemical content. Specific cars were dumped in to the ore dock pockets with the sequencing as specified by the steel companies.

Lump ore was always dumped into the pockets first due to the fact that if fines were on the bottom, the openings clogged, and ore would not flow into the boat. At times, steel companies required ore mixes involving mines located on different railroads. Consequently, Soo/NP ore was interchanged with the GN and DM&IR and occasionally Cuyuna range ore found its way to Two Harbors to be dumped. Similarly, Great Northern and DM&IR ore cars were occasionally seen on the NP dock in Superior.

Motive power for the yard and dock operations included the Soo Line's sole 2-10-0—the **950,** while the Soo's own Superior dock remained in operation. Starting in 1929, the **950** was sent to the Wisconsin Central dock at Ashland; Soo motive power was probably never used on the NP dock.

Besides the complex classification work in the yard, additional switching was needed to achieve the ordered blending by appropriately placing the car blocks over the ore dock pockets. Some blocks of cars could be as short as one or two cars, and occasionally

The Crosby depot was a 32 foot by 72 foot brick passenger station at the end of the Crosby trackage. Passenger trains had to back in before being able to proceed either west or east.
Pete Bonesteel Collection

When it is difficult to find photos of a particular piece of equipment, it is best to keep an eye for different photos, which may possibly have the subject of search as part of the photo. In this case, this photo of the Armour No. 1 includes a Summer's Ore Car to the left, series 80000 to 80199.

Pete Bonesteel Collection

an eight hour shift was used to place 150 cars. (Modern day taconite pellet ore dock dumping as on the BN and DM&IR require very little switching.)

By 1980 these complex operations had ended for the Soo crews and until 1984, loaded trains were delivered to the DM&IR for handling by that railroad's crew at their Duluth docks.

Superior Ore Dock.
Jan. 10-1918.

The dock had now been completed, and this photo, taken in 1918, shows the compete dock (2412 feet in length). Some might consider the dock a work of art, but in less than ten years, the facility would be in need of very expensive repairs. This was the major incentive to establish the pooling agreement with the Northern Pacific.

Stuart Nelson Collection

When the line from Iron Hub to Deerwood was abandoned, the first class Deerwood depot was moved to Riverton. It was an extensive operation as the depot was cut into several sections and loaded on flat cars. It required about eight cars to complete the move. On the flat car just behind the box car the station's outhouse roof can be seen lying on its side.

Stuart Nelson Collection

The Soo Line's Timber Ore Dock

The Soo's own ore dock was built 'hurry up' and resulting maintenance problems dogged operation of the structure throughout its brief life.

The dock was constructed in four stages. The first stage (built 1910-1911) was 600 feet long and had 50 '300 ton' capacity pockets on each side of the dock. As each pocket was built on 12 foot centers, the 24 foot ore cars would fit over 'every other pocket' for dumping purposes.

Expansion included a 600 foot extension completed in 1912, a third 600 foot addition in 1913, and a final extension 612 feet in length built during 1916-1917. The completed dock was thus 2412 feet long. There were 201 pockets on either side for a total capacity of 120,600 tons. This was the longest ore dock ever constructed on the Great Lakes. (The DM&IR's #6 dock was the largest with a capacity of 153,600 tons, however; it is 2304 feet in length.)

After the 1928 season, plans were made to dismantle the dock; razing began in 1929 and continued during 1930. Sadly, a fire destroyed what was left of the dock in September of 1930. Only a few pilings remain in 1994 to mark a once spectacular ore dock.

February 16, 1917   **Stuart Nelson Collection**

January 18, 1917   **Stuart Nelson Collection**

There was careful planning and execution of the piling for the third extension of the Soo's own ore dock on St. Louis Bay as these photos depict. The original section (built 1910-1911), however, was unstable in the soft mire of the bay because of hurried and inadequate planning. By 1925, it was apparent, that the dock would need extensive repairs, or perhaps be dismantled and replaced by an entirely new dock. This led to the ore pooling agreement with the Northern Pacific.

July 21, 1916   **Stuart Nelson Collection**

View of the Armour No. 1 mine, which operated from 1914 to 1959 by Inland Steel Company. Nearly 7,000,000 tons of ore were shipped from this mine.

Pete Bonesteel Collection

Mines of the Cuyuna

Algoma
Alstead
Armour Mine No. 1
Armour Mine No. 2
Carlson-Nelson
Croft
Curley Adams
Cuyuna Sultana
Evergreen
Feigh
Ferro
Gloria
Healy
Hillcrest
Hopkins Mine No. 1
Hopkins Mine No. 2
Huntington
Iron Mountain
Ironton and Pennington
Joan Mine No. 1
Joan Mine No. 3
Joan Mine No. 4
Kennedy

Liberty
Louise (ex-Cuyuna-Mille Lacs)
Mahnomen
Mangan Mine No. 1
Mangan Mine No. 2
Mangan Mine No. 3
Maroco
Martin
Meacham
Merritt Mine
Milford
New Clark
New Gloria
Northland
Portsmouth
Thompson
Evergreen
Proston
Rowe
Sagamore
Snowshoe
Wearne

(Mines in bold produced in excess of 900,000 tons of ore during their span of operation).

West 7th Avenue and Superior Street in 1910 – when the Soo Depot (ne Wisconsin Central) was new. Not an auto in sight! To the right we see Union Station and its train shed which is now the Lake Superior Transportation Museum.

The Twin Ports of Duluth and Superior lie at the far west end of Lake Superior. Duluth alone has about fifty miles of frontage in the harbor area. The city proper stretches out along the hilly North Shore for some twenty-five miles. Although it was settled initially about 1850 it grew like topsy during the 1880s and 1890s with the massive lumbering of the white pine forests and then with the discovery and exploitation of the iron ranges nearby. The Cuyuna Range near Crosby-Ironton was the last of the commercial ranges to ship ore and the Soo Line was the first line to serve the Cuyuna mines in 1911. The Soo had built its own ore dock in Superior across the Duluth harbor. This remarkable dock after several extensions became the longest, largest wood ore dock in the world before it was taken out of service in 1929.

The Port of Duluth serves as the western gateway for the St. Lawrence Seaway and there are many terminal elevators in the harbor with huge capacities served by the Soo.

Prior to the Soo Line merger of 1961 there were eight railroads directly serving Duluth/Superior (often times called the Twin Ports). They were the Minneapolis, St. Paul and Sault Ste. Marie, Northern Pacific, Great Northern, Duluth, Winnipeg and Pacific, the Milwaukee Road, Chicago and Northwestern, Duluth, Missabe and Iron Range and the Duluth, South Shore and Atlantic railroads. At that time there were three separate passenger terminals.

The GN, NP and the Soo had pool passenger agreements whereby a ticket on one line to the Twin Cities was honored by either of the other lines. In 1956, for instance, a round trip was $7.10 with service five

Painting by Russ Porter

Soo Line Train No.65 for Thief River Falls slumbers quietly overnight at the Duluth Soo Line Station. Elgin, Joliet and Eastern RR business car #40 rests nearby.

times each day. The Soo's 62-63 had air conditioned coaches but only the Great Northern's Gopher and Badger had a parlor-lounge car. Travel time was four hours fifteen minutes either way. In 1915 the Soo featured two trains each way over the Twin Ports - Twin Cities route. The day trains, 62-63, not only featured a parlor car but also a cafe-library-observation at the rear. Trains 64-65 had standard sleepers over the route at night.

Soo rails reached Duluth-Superior in 1909 from Onamia on the Brooten line and the following year the Plummer line reached Moose Lake. Fortuitously, in 1909 the Soo leased the Wisconsin Central which had already reached Superior from the south. The newly-leased road was finishing a magnificent depot on Duluth's Superior Street accessible by tunnel which served patrons until the Laker was discontinued to

Chicago. This was the Soo's finest and largest depot of its own and had six terminal tracks in a stub end arrangement.

Steel was king for years in this hilly lakeside city and there was even a U.S.Steel factory on the west side. Today shipping, including taconite from the Missabe Range, continues to be of major importance. Yet much employment centers about healthcare, education and tourism. The University of Minnesota-Duluth plus St. Scholastica and Wisconsin State University-Superior across the harbor provide excellent opportunities for thousands. The picturesque and inviting North Shore begins at Duluth and continues all the way to Thunder Bay. To the north is the Superior-Quietico Wilderness area on the boundary of Minnesota and Ontario.

Interior of the Soo's Duluth depot circa 1952. The airy grandùer of this depot (here one sees the main concourse) was not matched by any other Soo depot nor for that matter many depots of any line.

Leaving the Duluth depot and entering the tunnel.

Behind the ticket counter. (1953)

*Last day of steam on the Plummer Line.***2713** stopped at 21st street in Superior to change from steam to diesel for the run into Duluth. February, 1955

Coaling tower at the 21st street roundhouse area. A DSS & A Baldwin rests under the tower. January, 1955

557 at 21st street. June, 1956

The Soo Line continues to have significant yards and trackage in Duluth including the Rice's Point yard adjacent to the Port of Duluth as well as the Superior terminal. However; it can no longer reach the Twin Ports on its own rails. From Mineapolis-St. Paul today's Soo has trackage rights over the former Great Northern (BN). From Bemidji the Thief River Falls/Plummer traffic rides over the Burlington Northern also. These tracks were the former Great Northern route from Grand Forks to Duluth.

Only the western portion of the Brooten Line to Genola exists now and so the sole routes to Duluth-Superior from the Twin Cities and western points are the two Burlington Northern lines. A most tenuous and precarious situation at best, but the heavy traffic density does permit expenditures for better maintenance of the roadbed.

Fantastic is the best way to describe the Lake Superior Transportation Museum now housed in the former Union Station building in downtown Duluth—only a stone's throw away from the now razed Soo Line station. Interpreted exhibits along with dozens of well-preserved locomotives, work equipment and cars—both freight and passenger—bring to life the golden age of rails in the north of the North Star State.

Otto Dobnick

RICE'S POINT - The Port of Duluth was constructed on land purchased from the Soo Line. The primary rail access to the port is by the Soo Line. Port tonnage has increased somewhat steadily through the years but its use has never achieved the original rosy expectations.

Duluth is noted for its hills, bridges and railroad lines. Here we see a Soo Line transfer approaching the Grassy Point swing bridge after passing under the Interstate Highway bridge - September 1986.

Otto Dobnick

Duluth- looking southeast towards Superior with Interstate 35 in the foreground. The interstate bridge to Superior over the channel to St. Louis Bay dominates the righthand side of this photo. Rice's Point Soo Line yards are just to the left before the yards. (Note the proximity to the terminal grain elevators of the Port of Duluth). DM & IR tracks are next to the freeway in the foreground, and the BN's yard dominates the area just beyond the freeway. The DM & IR ore docks are off the photo to the right and beyond them (to the south) is the Grassy Point Bridge pictured below.

Frank King, photo. Wayne Olsen Collection

It's 1954 and No. 64 Eastbound from Thief River Falls is just over the Grassy Point Bridge by West Duluth. As with the other railroad bridges in the Duluth area, this is a center swing type. Note the combination RPO, baggage and passenger car consist on this run so typical of the latter years.

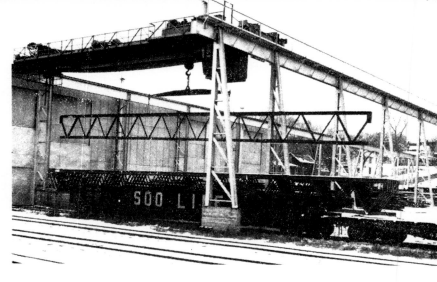

Steel for the Duluth Port Authority dock and warehouses was fabricated in St. Paul and travelled via the Soo over the Frederic-Dresser Line on hundreds of flats as pictured here (St. Paul, late 1950s).

Soo Line Railroad Collection

In May, 1959 the Port of Duluth officially received its first large salt water vessel (The Ramon de Larrinaga). This historic moment stemmed from a decision in 1953 by the Canadian government to go ahead with the St. Lawrence Seaway Project. Immediately, the United States also decided to join the effort which would bring large ocean going vessels to all of the Great Lakes. Thus the Seaway Port Authority of Duluth was organized with ten million dollars from state and local sources. This authority purchased some of the Soo Line's Rice's Point land holdings and developed nine berths, constructed two gantry cranes as well as some rather large warehousing facilities as shown at left.

Soo Line Railroad Collection

During a late afternoon in 1955 we see that No. 62 has arrived from the Twin Cities with a GP 9 at the point while No. 18, the Chicago bound Laker, waits for its power to arrive on track 1. It will have a 7 pm departure for its overnight journey to Chicago.

Wayne Olsen

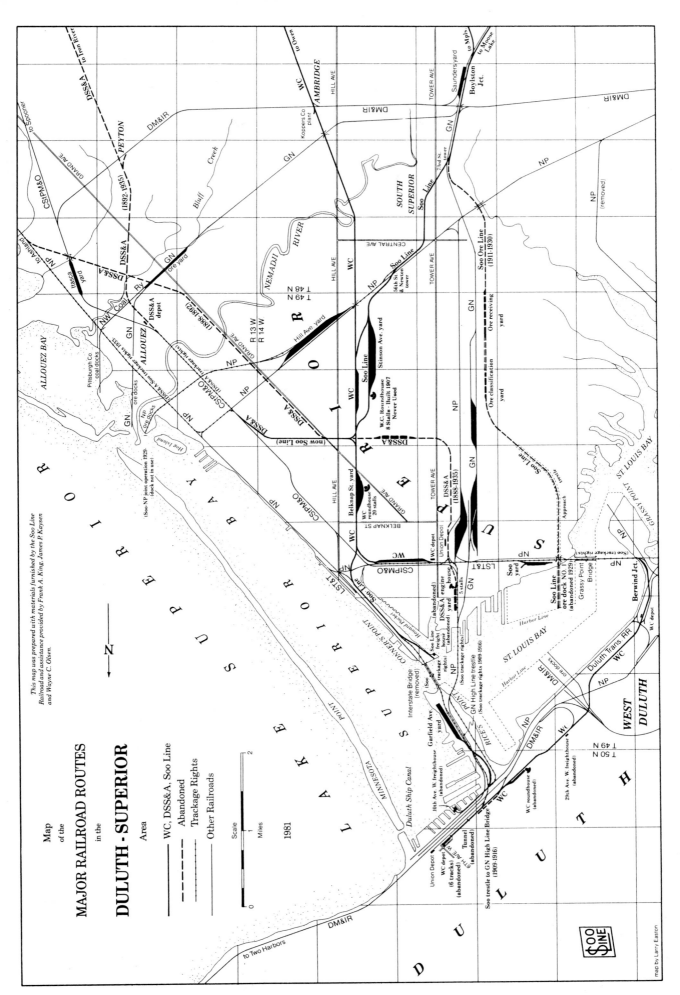

Map
of the

MAJOR RAILROAD ROUTES
in the

DULUTH · SUPERIOR

Area

1981

This map was prepared with materials furnished by the Soo Line
Railroad and assistance provided by Frank A. King, James P. Kaysen
and Wayne C. Olsen.

N

————	WC, DSS&A, Soo Line
– – – –	Abandoned
++++++	Trackage Rights
————	Other Railroads

Scale

Miles
0 1 2

map by Larry Easton

The above map was published in the July 1981 The Soo (the official publication of the Soo Line Historical and Technical Society) and is used with permission.

West Duluth

Above: The newly constructed West Duluth Depot at the foot of Ramsey Street (December 1916). It was torn down in 1992.

Left: The West Duluth Depot weathered well thanks to the brick and stone facing. It was still in Soo service throughout the 1970s. (Photograph taken December 9, 1961).

SAFETY

COURTESY

Mr. Ticket Agent:

THE FIRST STEEL TRAINS
INTO
DULUTH AND SUPERIOR
WERE *SOO LINE* TRAINS AND THE SERVICE TODAY IS AS PERFECT AS MODERN TRAIN SERVICE CAN BE.

2 DAILY TRAINS 2
ALL-STEEL, ELECTRIC-LIGHTED

YOUR PASSENGERS WILL APPRECIATE A TICKET VIA THE *SOO LINE*, SO WILL

J. A. McKINNEY, Traveling Passenger Agent
Robert and Fourth Sts.   ST. PAUL, MINN.

In April 1943 A.T. Erickson, general passenger agent of the Soo was informed by Walter Butler Shipbuilders, Inc of Superior that the Dione Quintuplets and their party would come to Superior to christian and launch five ships built at Butler's yard for the war effort.

A CP Standard sleeper (Glen type) 10 compartment car carried the official party from North Bay, Ontario and Soo business car 49 was at the rear of train 7/17 on Friday May 7, 1943. The ships were launched without incident but under tight security on May 8th and 9th and the party returned to Ontario on trains 18/8 the evening of May 9th..

This photo shows business car 49, the quints, Catherine Butler standing on the outside of the rear platform and Mr. and Mrs. Butler looking up at the quints.

No. 65 from Thief River Falls is seen arriving at Superior August 8, 1955. Engine **353** (an Alco RS 1 which had been on the Soo only eight months) is pulling the usual triple-car combination.

At Superior an H 1 light Pacific waits while mail and railway express is loaded for Minneapolis. Note that the station has a tile roof. The crossing tower was still in use during 1948 when E. Anderson preserved this scene.

Lake Superior Museum of Transportation

FA-1 units **210 A** and **B** head up a solid train of boxcars at Superior in November 1951. Note the two billboard boxcars with the four foot high billboard 'SOO LINE.' The Soo was among the first railroads to use the large lettering in 1950-51.

Soo Line Railroad

2118, an SW 9, was repainted into the attractive red white and blue livery about 1976. This engine was retired at Shoreham and rebuilt into a humpslug.

Soo Line Railroad

Close-up view of Alco FA-1 **2221A** at Superior, 12-14-62–just months before retiring from Soo rails in 1963. The trucks and GE traction motors from 22 of the 1500 hp Alco's were to ride under the new Soo's GP 30's which went into service in 1963.

Robert Anderson photo, Dennis Schmidt Collection

St. Paul to the Twin Ports

The following advertisement heralded the opening of the new line to Duluth in 1912. It was written by W.R. Callaway:

The completion of the new Twin City–Duluth–Superior Line has opened a new highway for comfortable travel between these cities. That part of the line from Minneapolis to Frederic has had a regular train service since 1901, and the country it traversed is well known, it being a rich farming and dairying district. The glimpses afforded of pastoral simplicity and content, of pretty little cottages nestling back into sheltering groves of hardwood; herds of peacefully grazing cattle and the bountiful fields; present a picture of happiness and plenty as to be a righteous cause of envy.

Beyond Frederic, the lake dotted almost virgin forest, will afford a treat to anyone whether or not acquainted with the primeval beauty of the northern parts of the wonderful states of Wisconsin and Minnesota. Mile after mile the pictures glide by, swiftly changing, always different, all of them fascinating in their personification of the peace, quiet and restfulness that nature alone in her most pleasant moods can create. The gemlike lakes on either hand glisten in the sunshine like polished mirrors, broken only by the leap of the black bass. The rippling, murmuring rills and creeks wandering apparently aimlessly through the natural meadows and under the sheltering branches of centuries old leafy monarchs, and filled with speckled beauties, are silver ribbons that the eye delights to follow until some turn of the track shuts them from view.

To the average traveler the journey is a revelation as to the possibilities of this territory and it will be but a short time when this route in its entire length will be through a thickly settled and prosperous dairy country.

With promotion like the above it can be understood that many a farm or town settler might be attracted to this area in hopes for better opportunity. Sadly enough, those pioneers of 1912 found no Red River Valley.

It should be noted that for sixty years prior to the construction of the Frederic Line there had been intense lumbering activity in the St. Croix Valley; the first commericial saw mill operation was at Marine on St. Croix in 1837. There have been 133 saw mills in operation over the years, with the peak years of white pine harvest occurring during the eighties.

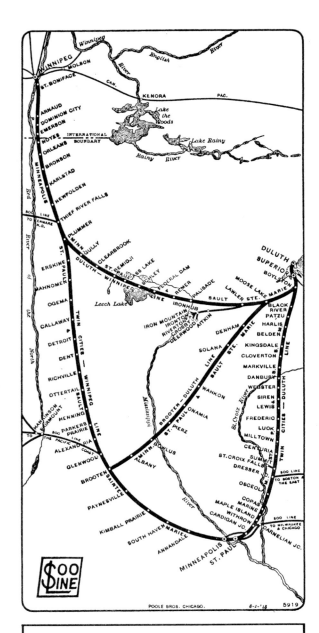

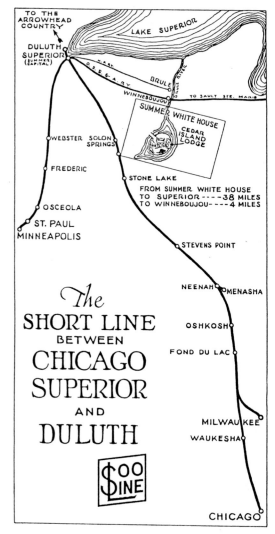

To The
Arrowhead
Country

LAKE SUPERIOR

DULUTH
SUPERIOR
(SUMMER
CAPITAL)

O.S.&G.Ry.

BRULE

WINNEBOUJOU

To Sault Ste. Marie

SUMMER WHITE HOUSE

CEDAR
ISLAND
LODGE

WEBSTER SOLON
SPRINGS

FREDERIC

STONE LAKE

FROM SUMMER WHITE HOUSE
TO SUPERIOR ---- 38 MILES
TO WINNEBOUJOU ---- 4 MILES

OSCEOLA

ST. PAUL
MINNEAPOLIS

STEVENS POINT

NEENAH   MENASHA

The
SHORT LINE
BETWEEN
CHICAGO
SUPERIOR
AND
DULUTH

OSHKOSH

FOND DU LAC

SOO LINE

MILWAUKEE

WAUKESHA

CHICAGO

July 4, 1906 Luck Wisconsin   Stuart Nelson Collection

The line was laid from St. Croix Falls to Frederic in 1901, but it was not completed to Duluth until 1911.

Stuart Nelson Collection

Cloverton, one of many towns carved out of the northern woods by the Soo, was touted as a dairy center, but the land was marginal to sustain even diversified agriculture. The author's mother taught here for two years back in 1920. Two passengers have just gotten off No. 63 which is continuing on to St. Paul and Minneapolis.

Although it is not the purpose of this book to discuss the Wisconsin Central Division or the Duluth South Shore and Atlantic, it is of general interest that in 1928 President Coolidge stayed near Superior. He travelled on the Soo's Frederic Line to Siren for a fishing outing. When the President went to Hibbing to inspect the iron mine there, a Soo Line Diner and crew accompanied the train.

An early fall afternoon in 1954. Soo train No. 63 is leaving Duluth for it's 168 mile run to Minneapolis. Round trip fare was but $6.75 and through tickets were honored inter-changeably on the Soo, the Great Northern, and the Northern Pacific. Note the Baldwin–type disk center driver on **727**.

Wayne Olson

The bridge at Marine, Minnesota had been destroyed by fire following a wreck in 1897. Very quickly, Soo forces rebuilt the timber bent span again over the St. Croix River with the above technique.

State Historical Society of Wisconsin

Siren, Wisconsin 1916 : Like so many towns along this line, Siren had a standard two-story 2nd class depot. Note the Western Express sign. This was the Soo's own express company.

Ed Wertman Collection

Above Left: The St. Croix Falls depot was at the end of a very short branch near Dresser, Wisconsin on the old St. Paul - Twin Ports Line. (1973)

Patrick Dorin

Left: Copas- This 16' X 48' depot even had a basement (built from standard plan 211). The agent was removed in 1931 as part of depression era cost containment. Note the mail crane at the end of the platform. (Circa 1940)

Stuart Nelson Collection

Minneapolis-bound way freight north of Dresser, WI during the early 1950s. **1017**, a Mikado from Superior, smokes up the countryside.

Dresser, WI during the late 1940's. The Soo had few Fairbanks-Morse coaling stations. Tenders could be served both on the main line as well as on the siding.

No. 62 is at the South Minneapolis yard on its way over Milwaukee Road trackage rights to St. Paul's Union Station. This morning train to the Twin Ports not only stops at Withrow, Marine, Dresser, and Frederic, but also at all points between with its mail, baggage, express, and passenger accommodation.

Right: At Bald Eagle, February 6, 1955 while waiting for a Northern Pacific special movement, onlookers get to watch Soo Line X4007E, a ski train special to Dresser.

The Winnipeg Line

Conception of the important third and central link of the Soo Line with the Canadian Pacific began in earnest in 1901-02 with economic planning both in Minneapolis and Montreal. The CP favored a route deep into the Red River Valley while Minneapolis favored a more easterly route. After T.I. Hurd made his survey and report in 1902, the route through Detroit (Lakes) was chosen.

Construction contracts for the Winnipeg Line-Glenwood to White Earth Indian Reservation (some 125 miles) were let in the spring of 1903 with the main contract going to Richards-Lundeen Company of Minneapolis. The actual contract was mainly for the grading. The railroad itself placed the ties and laid the rail. The Soo also received bids from Winston Brothers, P.O. Malley and Halverson and Richardson - all three of the firms were also from Minneapolis.

Richards-Lundeen had multiple crews grading at various spots simultaneously. From Glenwood to Alexandria the grading was rather simple and straight-forward as the line follows the west edge of an outwash plain with morraine hills being further to the west. After Alexandria, considerable difficulty was encountered because of the many lakes and swamps. In fact, from Alexandria to Carlos the line drops 58 feet in but seven miles. Attesting to the softness of the land, Soo forces battled to bring 200 feet of tie and rail back to grade when the new line slid into the muddy edge of Lake Irene. Just a few miles to the north an up grade of 63 feet in eight miles is encountered between Miltona and Parkers Prairie. The countryside near Parkers Prairie lies in and on the Leaf Hills range–the area exhibiting the tallest and grandest glacial morraines in Minnesota. A now abandoned branch line of the Northern Pacific was crossed at Henning and south of Detroit Lakes, the new line followed gently rolling sandy hills of an outwash plain. Rails reached Detroit (Lakes) during the fall of 1903 and the crew was tied up that winter.

The line had originally been conceived to go north from Detroit (Lakes) to White Earth, tribal head-quarters of the White Earth Band of the Chippewa, but because of terrain difficulties and problems concerning a clear title to the Indian lands, it was decided to run up the western edge of the reservation–through Waubun, Mahnomen and Ogema. Ogema was in a low lying swampy area and in fact not where any of the Native Americans had residence. (The origin of the Chippewa names for the reservation towns is described on page 58

Part I). Mahnomen (which means Wild Rice) is where the line crosses the Wild Rice River and where a roundhouse and turntable were placed. During the days of steam this was the crew change point.

South of Erskine, the tracks descend the Herman Beach of ancient Lake Agassiz. At Erskine the Soo crosses the Burlington Northern (former GN mainline between Grand Forks and Duluth). From Erskine and north to Winnipeg the track lies more or less in the Red River Valley, but several beaches of the glacial lake are crossed between Anita and Newfolden.

Thief River Falls became the Division point with roundhouse and shops. From here to the east was a small Soo owned railway, the Minnesota Northwestern Electric (chronicled in *Part I*). From Thief River and 300 miles to Kenmare, the Wheat Line was built in northwestern North Dakota during 1905. Actually, the conception of the Wheat Line was simultaneous with the Winnipeg Line. North from Thief River the road traverses rich farmland with potatoes, wheat, sugar beets and sunflowers being cropped today. Earlier it was a prosperous diversified area with much dairying.

Both Parkers Prairie and Alexandria were home to well known political figures. Following the Civil War, Knute Nelson eventually settled in Alexandria and was to become Governor of Minnesota. In 1895 he ran for Senate against W.D. Washburn (founding father of the Soo Line in 1883) and won with some perhaps not so silent backing of Jim Hill (Hill never forgot that the Soo tapped western Minnesota and North Dakota resources he felt his Great Northern deserved). Nelson went on to become one of Minnesota's greatest senators. Arthur Charles Townley grew up in Parkers Prairie and completed high school in Alexandria. He subsequently moved to Beach, ND and organized the Populist/Socialist Non-Partisan League among North Dakota farmers.

Today, both Mahnomen and the Thief River Falls area have large Indian gambling casinos which have brought a turnabout to the Native American fortunes along the line. Glenwood, the Alexandria area, Henning and the Detroit Lakes area are all blessed with excellent lakes with fine opportunities for vacations and renewal. Additionally, Alexandria, Detroit Lakes and Thief River Falls each have campuses of the Minnesota Technical College system. Prior to the 1990 acquisition of the Soo Line by the Canadian Pacific, the Winnipeg Line had greater traffic density than the Portal gateway which allowed the CP a longer haul. In 1995, far more tonnage crosses the International boundary at Portal than at Noyes/Emerson. Portal is the short way east.

State Historical Society of Wisconsin

In 1926, the Soo's depot was a busy place, even though the presence of the Great Northern (much closer to downtown–west and north of this view from the south) was dominant, and the Soo struggled here for long distance passenger revenues.

Below: Also in Alexandria, a grocery wholesaler is picking up the L.C.L. goods from the set out boxcar. Photo circa 1926.

State Historical Society of Wisconsin

During 1903 as the Soo extended its tracks north through Alexandria, the main line of the Great Northern needed to be crossed. Jim Hill would not allow a diamond. Thus the Soo under Pennington was forced to elevate its grade and build a timber crossing over the GN tracks as shown above. By 1956 these timbers were beginning to fail and the Soo elected to replace them with concrete piers. The right hand set of tracks above were taken out of service. Piling was driven and concrete forms were built. Concrete shuttles were constructed on section crew cars and ready mix concrete was brought to the site—eventually allowing construction of the piers as shown in the last photo below.

The Soo was to have the last laugh since the Burlington Northern (Great Northern) sold this line to the Otter Tail Valley Railroad. The line is now abandoned from St. Cloud to Fergus Falls and the grade serves as a snowmobile trail.

All photos: Bill Egan, Alexandria 1956

The original (1903) first class wooden Alexandria depot was burned in 1913 and replaced by the edifice below. Note the horse-drawn hack. Alexandria is the county seat of Douglas county in the heart of Minnesota's prime lake country.

Douglas City Historical Society

1922: Northbound local arrives at the pristine brick veneer first class Alexandria depot which served the city at its eastern edge until passenger service was discontinued in 1967. The depot itself was razed in 1980 after attempts to donate it to the city and area technical school had failed.

Douglas City Historical Society

December 1951: looking south at Alexandria. The Soo proudly proclaimed its presence with the neon dollar sign, but had only one first class passenger train a day north and south. Travelers going to the west coast had to travel 20 miles south to Glenwood to catch the Dominion. The Great Northern, with its depot to the west and close to the business district, had the lion's share of Alexandria passenger business with the Western Star, the Red River, and the Winnipeg Ltd.

Richard Anderson

Ed Wertman Collection

Daytrain North. Wooden coaches and Soo Standard **43** Northbound at Carlos. The engine crew, conductor, and trainman are all standing still as the engine while the photographer keeps this day for us.

Douglas County Historical Society

1918: The troops return from the 'War to end all Wars'

Pete Bonesteel

Right: Ottertail 1910. A brass band, and the fire brigade all await a long forgotten politician. That's a Soo Standard 4-4-0 going south off the photo.

Pete Bonesteel Collection

Only 10 GP 38-2's were delivered with the bold 'Soo' in <u>red.</u> 790-799 came to the road during 1977 and 1978; all units thereafter reverted to 'Soo' in black. See page 196 for an unscheduled activity of 791 shown above.

1911 Parkers Prairie view of depot and lumberyard looking west. The outhouse is north on the right. Note the barrels in front of the lumber yard.

Pete Bonesteel Collection

Right: southbound (eastward) way freight waits for clearance. July 1958

Stuart Nelson Photo

Ogema-about 1910 in the heart of the White Earth Indian reservation. Today a quiet and dwindling farming community, this view from the North shows the wind mill and water tower. Note the very long wooden passenger platform.

James Richards Collection

On the bottom of page 41 in *Saga of the Soo Part I* is a view of Ogema from the south showing the yard and a southbound passenger train.

Below: Waubun business section in 1905–looking west. Some of the store buildings are still under construction and are not yet painted. The elevator on the left is the 'Prairie Elevator' and to its left is apparently a hotel. Note also the lumber yard. The elevator on the right is the Woodworth, a small 'line company' that was active until perhaps twenty years ago.

John Hall Collection

Above: 'humpback' timber road trestle over Soo tracks north of Detroit Lakes near Westbury. At one time there were countless trestle grade crossings similar to the above, but high maintenance and wintertime snow plow nightmares have dwindles their ranks.

Northbound local No. 111 with Soo Standard **28** on the point circa 1904 at Detroit Lakes. Note the stockpiled ties–all aboard.

For further coverage of Detroit Lakes, see page 40 *Part I.*

Some engineers plow snow, but Ray Rambeck rides GP 38-2 **791** and GP 30 **721** into the dirt at Mahnomen. Said Ray: "You run out of railroad in a hurry on a day like this." The switch had been tampered with and a special investigator caught the kids who had opened the turnout.

Winton Forsberg

Pete Bonesteel

1914: Waiting for the southbound at Callaway–originally Baxter.

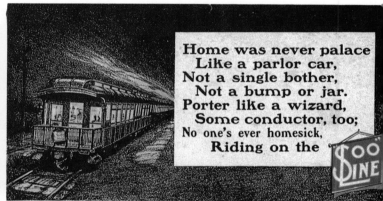

Home was never palace
Like a parlor car,
Not a single bother,
Not a bump or jar.
Porter like a wizard,
Some conductor, too;
No one's ever homesick,
Riding on the "Soo"

Ron Olin Collection

Note the stub switches looking north to the roundhouse. The depot is on the left and the coal dock is on the extreme right before the water tank. Today, Mahnomen farmers' grain has an enormous elevator complex west of the main and, of course, the 'Shooting Star' Chippewa casino is in full operation to the south of where this photo was taken. (See also page 41 in *Part I*).

Al Ohrt Collection

SOO YARDS. MAHNOMEN, MINN.

Caboose and more...

Lloyd Berger, Jr.

Yes, there indeed is a one spot. Lloyd Berger caught it during an early snow, November 9, 1973, at Thief River Falls.

Lloyd Berger, Jr.

99100—one of the unique transfer caboose designs to be found. This was at Superior, June 17, 1972.

Why cannot a caboose show its faces? If it belongs to the Soo Line many possibilities exist. Take your pick, sad, happy, or in between. I doubt, however, that the brass would like a moustache in linear service, Hankinson and west!

Gerald Olson

In 1995, the caboose has become a vanishing breed, all but extinct. Only in situations where lengthy backup moves are made is the railroad willing to pull the extra fifteen or twenty tons. One example of a 'modern need' for a caboose would be the movements and interchange at Minot. Taking cars to and from the Burlington Northern at Gavin Yard requires a backup of four to five miles. The last new caboose(s) were delivered in November 1974 from International Car. They were numbered 106-145. At this time the Soo does not do maintenance on any of their caboose(s). This accounts for their current rusty appearance.
For more portraits of a variety of caboose(s) please see pages 168-69 *Part I*.

Boys and trains: from early times trains have served as special objects for young males' admiration. In the midst of World War II a Soo composite gondola is hauling scrap

Soo Line Historical and Technical Society

A walking plow rests on the platform awaiting pickup at Hazel - the first town south of TRF. Postcard view from about 1912.

Ron Olin Collection

WX2403–the X-1 outfit at Erskine on the way south (eastbound) to Ottertail (8-14-63). **2403** - a GP 9 outshopped by La Grange, December 1954. New Soo # **4212**

Stuart Nelson

Stuart Nelson Photo

No. 126 with largely newsprint as well as one car of Canadian livestock gets a highball from operator at 'RK' tower in Erskine, Autumn 1957.

Erskine, August 1963. By now the Erskine depot had been shortened as business declined, but note the fact that cream shipments are still regular.

Stuart Nelson

PLUMMER

an archetype country elevator

The Plummer elevator fortunately has survived to the present time without a great deal of external changes. Its history goes back to 1906 when a farmers' cooperative incorporated to provide a market outlet in this new town along the Winnipeg line which had been constructed in 1904. Compared to the lush prairies of the Red River Valley, the surrounding farm country would only be somewhat better than marginal. Therefore, the co-op did not succeed and it was sold to the then manager Andrew Gunderson. In 1942, Olaf Skatvold purchased the building and business. Seeing a need for livestock feed, Skatvold added a feedmill and actually enlarged it after the end of the war. In 1947, a seed cleaning plant was added that allowed local farmers to have their own grain cleaned for seed purposes. The photo below depicts the improved elevator in 1948.

At that time the common fuel for domestic and commercial heating was coal brought to the elevators' coal bins by boxcars on the Soo. From 35 to 40 carloads would be handled in Plummer each year. One could say that the typical country elevator at the mid-century mark was a multi-pointed service organization. All this was to change over a rather short interval as farmers rapidly undiversified and abandoned livestock feeding. Seed companies with disease resistant hybrid and registered or certified seed stock prospered because the yields were better. Finally, coal was no longer preferred as propane gas and fuel-oil became abundant and relatively inexpensive.

So, the coal sheds have been razed, the seed cleaning plant scrapped and the feed mill dismantled -

but in 1994 the elevator is still prospering. An extension to the cribbing has raised the height some twenty feet and the scale was changed to accomodate semi-trailer grain trucks. Although storage capacity is not dramatically greater, the yearly movement through this little elevator has increased ten-fold over the last fifty years. In 1943 some 350,000 bushels were handled. In the nineties 3,500,000 to 4,000,000 bushels are being handled each year. The present owner is the St. Hilare Farmers' Elevator Company.

Transportation of CROPS

The grain movement is of such vital concern that the Soo Line is doing its utmost to meet the challenge of a serious car shortage beyond our control. In cooperation with shippers of other commodities, we of the Soo Line are striving to achieve the most efficient use of all available equipment by urging a program which includes:

1. **Prompt unloading of all cars, including week-ends and holidays**

2. **Prompt notification to the railroad when an emptied car is available**

3. **Loading of cars promptly and to full capacity, and furnishing billing information quickly**

A continuance of the splendid cooperation you have given in the past will do much to aid in the accomplishment of our purpose and will be very much appreciated.

For shipping information, see your local Soo Line agent

AN INTERNATIONAL RAILROAD SYSTEM

$OO $INE

DETROIT LAKES RECORD - AUG. 1946

Prior to delivery artistic license is oftentimes used as in the above paint proposal for EMD GP 30 locomotives. Note the Blomberg trucks.

Lloyd Berger, Jr.

GP30 -- **707**; one of an order of 22 such units purchased in 1963. These General Motors 2250 horsepower units were all delivered to the Soo during 1963 in the red/white/black as shown. They are remarkable in that they rode on used Alco trucks from the traded-in FA units originally purchased in 1948. The Soo sold the serviceable units to the Wisconsin Central in 1987.

Caboose and more...

Lloyd Berger, Jr.

Yes, there indeed is a one spot. Lloyd Berger caught it during an early snow, November 9, 1973, at Thief River Falls.

Lloyd Berger, Jr.

99100–one of the unique transfer caboose designs to be found. This was at Superior, June 17, 1972.

Why cannot a caboose show its faces? If it belongs to the Soo Line many possibilities exist. Take your pick, sad, happy, or in between. I doubt, however, that the brass would like a moustache in linear service, Hankinson and west!

Gerald Olson

In 1995, the caboose has become a vanishing breed, all but extinct. Only in situations where lengthy backup moves are made is the railroad willing to pull the extra fifteen or twenty tons. One example of a 'modern need' for a caboose would be the movements and interchange at Minot. Taking cars to and from the Burlington Northern at Gavin Yard requires a backup of four to five miles. The last new caboose(s) were delivered in November 1974 from International Car. They were numbered 106-145. At this time the Soo does not do maintenance on any of their caboose(s). This accounts for their current rusty appearance.
For more portraits of a variety of caboose(s) please see pages 168-69 *Part I*.

Boys and trains: from early times trains have served as special objects for young males' admiration. In the midst of World War II a Soo composite gondola is hauling scrap

Soo Line Historical and Technical Society

A walking plow rests on the platform awaiting pickup at Hazel - the first town south of TRF. Postcard view from about 1912.

Ron Olin Collection

WX2403–the X-1 outfit at Erskine on the way south (eastbound) to Ottertail (8-14-63). **2403** - a GP 9 outshopped by La Grange, December 1954. New Soo # **4212**

Stuart Nelson

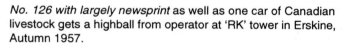

Stuart Nelson Photo

No. 126 with largely newsprint as well as one car of Canadian livestock gets a highball from operator at 'RK' tower in Erskine, Autumn 1957.

Erskine, August 1963. By now the Erskine depot had been shortened as business declined, but note the fact that cream shipments are still regular.

Stuart Nelson

Interesting here is the caboose 'filling station' at the Thief River yards 5-1-74.

800–first in its class of ten General Electric 3000 horsepower six-motored 430C freight locomotives at Thief River Falls 10-1-70. These engines were new in 1968.

Thirty-one below zero–February 1994 near Newfolden. Southbound No. 560

July 3, 1991: the Explorers Special eastbound is leaving North Dakota on the Wheat Line at the Oslo bridge (See *Part I* page 46 for other photos of this swing bridge). Special movement passenger trains on branch lines are indeed rare.

Thief River Falls

This division point city has always been important to Soo Line operations and although the Soo arrived here later than did the Great Northern, from the start (during 1904) it has always been the dominant rail service to the community. Even though the railroad employment today is way down, the town has remained prosperous and continues to grow. See page 42 *Part I* for more photos.

Pennington County Historical Society

A view from the west of the Kenyon designed depot. It is one of a handful of specially designed Soo depots and the classic structure stands yet today, but has been on the endangered list for several years and Thief River community folk are attempting to raise money to refurbish it. Let us hope it stands for many years yet. A photo of the depot under construction is found in Part I.

Percy Lamb photo, W.L. Lamb collection

Thief River, being the division point, saw almost all the classes of Soo motive power. Here are two examples of Class H-2: rare in that there were only four in this class, all built in 1910 and both photos date from 1910 in the Thief River yards.

A general view of the Thief River yards with the original first depot. Photo was likely taken from atop the car shop.

Pennington County Historical Society

At the close of the steam era—the south end of Thief River Falls looked as left—looking towards the freight depot. Tracks left to right: Electric Line, coal dock, house lead 1–2, coach rip 2, rip 1 (with Caboose) main and yard track. Spring 1956

Both photos:Millard Nelson Collection

Thief River yard looking northwest: rip track office is in the central foreground with the roundhouse leads off to the right. Look far and your imagination will take you to Noyes—80 miles north.

Thief River Falls was first seen by the Italian/French adventurer Beltrami, who left a U.S. Army expedition party on its way to Winnipeg in 1823. Beltrami worked his way back to Fort Snelling via one of the 'sources' of the Mississippi River.

The name Thief River or Robber River came from a renegade Sioux who hid himself near the river and its falls and robbed both fellow Sioux and Chippewas–always evading capture.

In 1888 the Red Lake River (which flowed out of the nearby Red Lakes) was dammed, allowing construction of a flour mill and a saw mill. Later, there was to be a steam powered flour mill which was constructed by one J. W. Howes. It is of historical interest that this same Howes also built a steam powered boat 'the Monitor' which plied both the Red Lake and the Thief Rivers. The Red Lake River was navigable upstream as far as the Indian agency on the Red Lake.

In 1892, commerce and travel were improved immensely by the arrival of the Great Northern. By the time the Soo Line arrived in 1904, Thief River Falls had become and remained the largest community on the

Winnipeg Line. The Soo really did play the major transportation role here with its 14-stall roundhouse and a Division point for the former Winnipeg Division. Very soon the railroad was well enough organized in this Pennington County community that it served as the eastern marshalling point for the 'Wheat Line' which was flung some 300 miles west to Kenmare during the 1905 construction season.

With the construction of the Duluth Line in 1909 and 1910, Soo tracks reached out in all directions. The little Minnesota Northwestern Electric Railway was to run some 18 miles east from Thief River to Goodridge. This line (completed in 1914) was a separate corporation but owned by the Soo. A General Electric motor car provided the little line's sole motive power until abandonment came in 1940. See pp 126-27 *Part I* for more details. From 1918 until 1926 car shops at the Thief River yard were very busy rebuilding and upgrading the Soo's wooden boxcar fleet. With the advent of composite box cars that were sturdier, the need for extensive rebuilds of all wooden cars waned and the program was discontinued.

Above: ALCO 1500 horsepower freight locomotive **208B** in the original maroon and gold scheme of the Minneapolis, St. Paul and Sault Ste. Marie RR with GP 9 **402** and a DSS&A Baldwin behind (all in pre-merger colors) at Superior. Photo taken April 23, 1962.

Right: **1003** Mikado has been pulled out of the Superior roundhouse for photos during a Soo Line Historical and Technical Society tour in the fall of 1987. Troubles with the flues prevented the further restoration and firing of this venerable old steamer. During 1994, however, the engine was moved and new flues have been fabricated. Under the sponsorship of the Wisconsin Railway Preservation Trust of Osceola WI, it is hoped to have this engine restored and under steam in short order.

Left: Four sisters under the skin with four paint schemes—each at Superior, September 10, 1993. **6056** in the last candy apple red scheme introduced by the Soo in 1989. CP Rail **3017** is in its 1980s scheme. **4437** is in the post merger white, red and black and trailing behind is an SD 40-2 painted in the new CP Rail America scheme adopted after the 1990 purchase of the Soo by the Canadian Pacific.

Charles Bohi

A study in tranquility: Train No. 560 crosses the Red Lake River at Thief River Falls behind **6005**, an SD 60 delivered in 1987. Photo taken July 11, 1992.

Westbound No. 65 arriving in Thief River on an early summer day, 1950. Notice the single-triple combine in tow. These cars were purchased from Georgia Car and Locomotive following use on the Chesapeake and Ohio. They saw many more years of service on low-density lines where the Soo had the U.S. Mail contract. Interstate highways propelled the Postal Service into using trucks, and without the subsidy a mail car rendered, the retail providing of passenger service was disastrously unprofitable. Now the roads are wearing out — rather like "the battle was won, but the war was lost."

A broadside view of this same car shows the six-wheel trucks and the monitor roof line. These cars were steam heated. In the diesel era they were best used in summer unless the locomotive had a steam generator as did some GP 9s.

Photograph by Stuart J. Nelson

Photograph by Stu Nelson

Soo Standard 4-4-0's were typical power on the Plummer Line to Duluth up through the 1920s. For a period of time there was also a night train each way with sleeper accommodations and connections to Winnipeg. This postcard view shows No.162 crossing the bridge at Thief River. Note the logs floating downstream upstream on the Red Lake River to the lumber mill which had been in operation from before the Soo Line era.

Pete Bonesteel Collection

205

Snow

Soo Line Railroad

Cleaning switches in the Glenwood yard. Hand labor is a necessity. 1971

In the Upper Midwest the solid form of H_2O is a given most winters, though the depth, stickiness and blizzard conditions may vary greatly from year to year. Annual snowfall in Soo Line Minnesota averages 40 to 48 inches a year, but in the Duluth/Moose Lake area that would be an underestimate.

Sometimes the traditional Russell plow or flanger cannot cope or do the necessary removal as the top photos of these two pages illustrate.

Snow scenes can also be found on pages 16, 34, 43, 44, 45, 50, 55,76, 93, 94, 103, 111, 112, 113, 123, 126, 154, 160, 161, 184, 187 and 191 in this volume as well as on pages 28, 29, 75, 129, 132, 133, 162 and 157 in *Saga of the Soo Part I.*

Truly, no railroad in the Upper Midwest has a shortage of the 'white stuff' but streamlining the grade cuts (started during the years following World War II and continuing to a limited extent today) has allowed blizzard winds to dump their 'harvest' in areas other than the right of way.

Left: mixed train on the Drake Line in 1950. The crew had to melt snow for engine water and the stranded crew and passengers received their meals at a nearby farm.

James Welton Collection

Soo Line Railroad

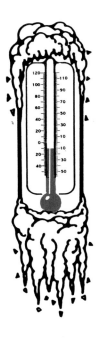

The winter of 1969 dumped an unmanageable amount of snow in and on the Wendell cut. An ingenious solution was to evolve in this post-rotary era. A crawler power shovel was mounted atop a flat car as shown above. The following summer found engineering crews supervising the movement of 300,000 cubic yards of dirt. The remodelled cut now allows blizzard winds to blow the tracks clear of snow.

All photos: Soo Line Railroad

Soo box cars have been among the most distinctive and attractive in the industry. This 50 footer with its red plug door seems almost festive in the snow.

The small yellow building in the center is the combination yard office & scale house. Behind is the trainmen's locker room. The Soo's ice house can be seen on the right. Thief River Falls Yard spring 1956.

Millard Nelson

No. 126 has just arrived from Noyes. The Thief River switch engine (Baldwin **367**) begins its task of classifying the train and adding cars for its trip to Glenwood and on to Minneapolis. Summer 1955.

Millard Nelson Collection   Photograph by Stu Nelson

View of the coaling tower from the southwest -- Thief River 1956. Note the sanding spouts and the water tower in the background. The engine is headed south (eastward) on the outgoing lead. The pump house is behind the engines.

Speed

PLUS

ETERNAL VIGILANCE

That's the watchword of Soo Line Service!

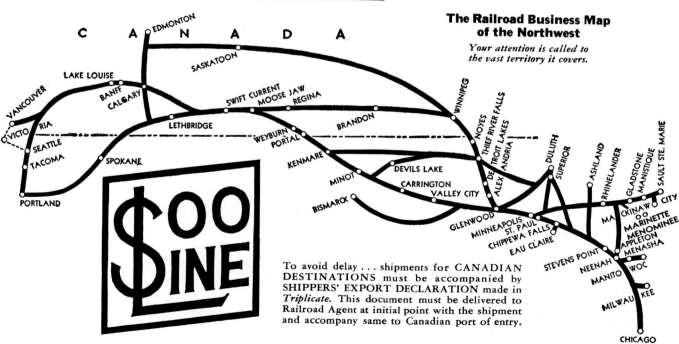

The Railroad Business Map of the Northwest

Your attention is called to the vast territory it covers.

To avoid delay . . . shipments for CANADIAN DESTINATIONS must be accompanied by SHIPPERS' EXPORT DECLARATION made in *Triplicate.* This document must be delivered to Railroad Agent at initial point with the shipment and accompany same to Canadian port of entry.

SOO SERVICE WILL BE SATISFACTORY TO YOU

Immigrants, Sod and Steel:
the World Reaches Newfolden

by John R. Tunheim

The Soo Line's later arrival meant that the railroad often bisected immigrant communities that for many years had existed in areas far from the larger towns adjoining earlier railroads. The 1880s and the 1890s marked a period during which extraordinary numbers of immigrants, particularly from northern Europe, settled in farming areas later to be served by the Soo. These prairie lands were a chief component of America's frontier at the time–tough, partially-wooded grasslands available free to immigrants who were willing to break the sod, build homes and create communities while enduring harsh winters and extreme isolation.

The northern Europeans were drawn by the promise of 160 acres of free land, an economic amenity unimaginable in their crowded homelands, and by friends' exaggerated descriptions of a paradise in the American heartland. They endured the hazards of rough trans-Atlantic journeys, confusing immigration centers, and long rides on railroads to towns that were but unfamiliar names scribbled on pieces of paper. There, unless friends were waiting for them, they visited the federal land office to copy maps and to inquire where their countrymen were settling. To the arriving immigrants, the best locales were the lands where people spoke their native tongue, where there were both wooded areas and open prairie, and where there were natural waterways and sandridges for easy transportation. It could be difficult to find available land in a roadless wilderness often a day's journey or more from the railroad; deciding which parcel was suitable for home and farm could also be a challenge. Often, the new arrivals camped in the area and constructed crude huts before families and belongings were carted across the marshes and trails.

Under the terms of the Homestead Act, citizens or aliens intending to become citizens were permitted to file claim on 160 acres of the public domain. The immigrant needed only to pay a small fee and swear that the land was for personal settlement and cultivation. After residing on the tract for five years, cultivating a portion of the land and making other improvements, the homesteader could apply for the patent, or title to the land. Naturalization as a United States citizen was required before an immigrant could secure title. New arrivals could also shorten the time requirement by paying the government $1.25 an acre or purchase land beyond the homestead under the Pre-Emption Law for the same price. In reality, many waited years before finally acquiring title to the land. As long as the claim was filed, the interest was protected and the many legal steps necessary for 'proving the claim' could be postponed. There was little concern in isolated communities that ownership interests would be challenged.

Immigrants tended to settle in ethnic enclaves, preferring to share the frontier experience with their fellow Norwegians, Germans, Swedes, Finns, Poles or other nationalities. Cultivating the prairie sod for the first time, building homes, creating new communities and assimilating into American life was made slightly easier with the help of people who shared a common language, customs and beliefs. Rather than being tossed immediately into the American melting pot, immigrants living in isolated ethnic communities chose the opportunity to assimilate more slowly and as a result, old world customs changed at a very gradual pace. The newcomers may have lacked in amenities and contact with the outside world, but they had the support and companionship of neighbors sharing the same experience.

LOCATION OF NEWFOLDEN AND NEW FOLDEN TOWNSHIP

Houses were initially crude dugouts or sod huts and later, if a wood supply was plentiful, small log cabins were constructed. These communities were self-sufficient, growing garden crops, making furniture and sewing clothes. Homes were insulated with clay and moss, and heated by wood cook stoves in the winter. Although some used candles for lighting at first, the safer kerosene lamp was widely used in the 1880s on the frontier. The lamps were used sparingly, and one household could get by on about five gallons of kerosene a year. Mattresses were filled each fall with fresh straw. Generally, in most areas the surface water supply was close to the ground so wells were relatively easy to dig. The well shaft was usually encased in stone and water was drawn by bucket or a long pole. The stone well shafts with cool air rising from the water below were the primary means of refrigeration for perishables such as milk, cream, and butter in the warmer months. Children were born in the homes with the help of a midwife. With doctors so far away the infant mortality rates along with general mortality from undiagnosed sickness were high. To be sure the medicine of the 1890s was seldom curative.

There was much back-breaking work that faced the settlers intent upon turning their homestead into a farm. Axes and grub hoes were used to clear brush, handdug ditches cleared water away, and one-bottom plows pulled by oxen slowly broke the tough virgin sod. Whatever equipment was available was shared among neighbors, but methods of planting, cultivating and harvesting the small grain crops remained crude for many years. Gradually, horses and rudimentary horse-drawn equipment made farming somewhat easier. Harvesting wheat and oats progressed from the scythe and hand-tied bundles to the reaper and later to the binder. Threshing began with horse-powered machines or sweeps and later progressed to the steam engine that travelled throughout the communities powering the threshing machines. Much of the grain produced was at first used for subsistence with wheat ground into flour for bread and oats used for animal feed; the relative lack of quality roads and excessive distances made it impractical to market grain.

Foods were homegrown staples: bread, garden crops, milk, eggs and butter. Farm animals also provided an important source of meat which was preserved by drying, salting or smoking. Abundant wildlife was used as an additional source of meat. Similarly, fish were taken from the rivers and berries were harvested each summer. Only items such as sugar, spices, coffee, molasses, syrups and yeast had to be purchased. Settlers could earn extra money by working on larger farms as hired help, selling eggs, milk and butter, or selling cattle. Sewing and knitting brought extra cash as did older children working on farms or as housemaids. Credit was virtually unavailable to the immigrant and as a result, very little money was available for improvements.

At first, only the high dry ridge land was used as trails. Travel was difficult, particularly in the winter. Fire was always a potential hazard to be reckoned with, especially prairie fires which effortlessly raced across the native prairies in years of drought. Many settlers ploughed wide firebreaks around their buildings to try to protect them from the devastation of fire.

During the early years of settlement by the Europeans, there were many Native American people in settled areas living off the land much like their ancestors had done. A succession of treaties opened up new areas for white settlement, but early arrivals encountered many Native American people. There was rarely conflict, and the Europeans and Native Americans learned over time to be of assistance to one another, despite difficulties in communication.

Part of the process of assimilating immigrant communities involved creating community institutions. Communities were self-governed and created townships that built roads and bridges. The enormous task of transforming a wilderness of trails into graded roads along section lines was accomplished over time, largely through the labor of the residents who were assesed at least one day's work each year as a 'poll tax' in order to construct the graded roads.

In the late 1800s, much of the area was covered with a vast network of small country post offices, many in farmhouses. With no system for rural mail delivery, many post offices were needed to distribute the U.S. Mail. Carriers were hired to irregularly deliver mail to and from the larger towns to these country offices. Postmasters were appointed by the President and served their neighbors through fourth class post offices bearing colorful names often reflecting memories of the old country. These post offices were social centers where neighbors visited when the mail arrived and cultural centers where the first news from the outside world arrived in an era of primitive communications.

The immigrants' churches mirrored the religious institutions of their homelands. Native languages were used exclusively in the churches until after the first generation was gone. These churches were the center of the community, a place where ethnic traditions could survive due in part to America's tolerance of religious freedom. On the other hand,

schools hastened the assimilation of the immigrant families in that children were required to learn and speak English, a language that they taught to their parents over time. Education was important to the immigrants and in isolated areas, the schools probably played the strongest role in the great, gradual transition of foreign-speaking immigrants into English-speaking American citizens.

Small country stores were opened by settlers to earn money as well as to convenience their neighbors. They carried a small inventory of daily needs and minimized the need for long trips to the railroad towns. They provided outlets for homegrown perishables such as milk, butter and eggs. These small trading posts were known as 'inland stores,' because they were located 'inland' from the railroads. Eventually, small inland villages grew up around these stores which usually included a post office and a blacksmith. Inland villages as such served only a small community and were therefore limited in their roles as economic centers. Most often located on someone's farm, the inland village was not a population center, but rather the rudimentary prelude to the commercial center of an isolated area.

Gradually, these tiny ethnic communities grew, and more immigrants continued to come. As roads improved, the communities grew closer to the outside

world and immigrants felt more comfortable in this new world frontier which was now their home. But the economic lifeblood of that era was the railroad. Graded roads of the horse and buggy era were no competition for the iron horse. No matter how much progress was made in developing an area, citizens were acutely aware of the importance of living in proximity to the railroad, both for economic development and for ease of life.

New Folden Township, in central Marshall County, Minnesota, was a typical Scandinavian ethnic community whose inhabitants assimilated slowly into American life. The immigrants began arriving in 1882 and for the next two decades, the community grew at a slow, measured pace, roughly one day's journey from Argyle or Warren, cities along the route of the St. Paul, Minneapolis and Manitoba Railroad, completed in 1878. Later called the Great Northern, this transportation artery was the settler's link to the outside world. New Folden residents naturally dreamed of having a railroad nearer to their community and for two decades, rumors spread quickly that a railroad was coming in their direction.

In 1901, the Soo and the Jim Hill's Great Northern planned northern extensions which would cross Native American lands that were soon to be opened. New lands and new settlements meant profits for railroads and the competition was intense. By 1903, the

Panoramic view of Newfolden circa 1916.

NEWFOLDEN

settlers in isolated New Folden Township received word that the Soo Line and the Great Northern would bisect each other at Thief River Falls and continue north, meaning a railroad would be coming much closer to the New Folden Township. By the summer of 1903 surveying crews were the first sign of the approaching railroad. Originally, the road had been projected north through an inland community called Pelan in Kittson County. The Soo Line's competition with the Great Northern for the fastest route to Winnipeg forced a change to a more direct route north. Pelan was doomed, and a town farther to the west, Karlstad was created instead.

By the autumn in 1903, the New Folden citizens watched with great anticipation as Soo surveyors platted the route with grade projections and bridges marked by numbered stakes. Exceeding everyone's anticipations, Great Northern survey crews were planning a route through central Marshall County a scant two miles east of New Folden Township. Landowners began selling right-of-way to the Soo's advance agent.

In the summer of 1904, the first construction crews arrived and began cutting down trees, grubbing and cleaning the land for the right-of-way. The summer was very rainy and the difficult job of grading the right-of-way proceeded slowly with horse-drawn scrapers and crews of men with spades and wheelbarrows. The steam shovels dug through the sandridges to level the grade but the work in the wetlands was done mostly by hand. The gravel trains followed on temporary trackage. A special crew built the bridge over the Middle River with the help of local men. Other crews worked on the depot and the telegraph lines. Area residents watched with amazement and let the work crew cooks use their kitchens and the crew members use their barns for sleeping. Next came the ties and then the huge machine that laid the gleaming eighty-pound steel rails. By October 26, 1904, the Winnipeg Line was completed to Emerson and supply trains began stocking the new settlements.

The new railroad passed within twenty rods of New Folden Township's 'inland town,' seemingly a logical place for a depot. The settlement was in the center of the township, had a post office and store, and was a popular gathering point. The Soo Line, however, chose an undeveloped site two miles north of the inland town where the Middle River crossed the roadbed. The site was marshy and as a result, could not be used for farming. The land was purchased less expensively and being built along the Soo Line. Such a 'foreign' name was considered unacceptable by the citizens and in the end the Soo Line agreed to name the new village 'Newfolden.'

On November 21, 1904, the entire township turned out to watch as a Soo Line passenger train passed through the township on its maiden voyage from St. Paul to Winnipeg. To many accustomed to a slower pace of life, it seemed a miracle that in one short year's time an entire railroad was built and the isolation of New Folden Township was ended. The noisy, thundering, smoky engine moved across the prairie at an unbelievable speed carrying passengers from the big cities through their tiny Scandinavian community. By the summer of 1905, the town of Newfolden had become a 'boom town' with fourteen new businesses, including hotels, butcher shops, general stores, restaurants, a lumber yard, grain elevators and a bank. The inland town became an immediate ghost town and Newfolden was now the town where people came from miles around to trade their moreover, the Soo Line was able to control the development of the town. The community did not fight that decision, but the following one was met with defiance. The Soo announced that the name of the new town on the banks of the Middle River would be 'Baltic,' in honor of the Baltic Elevators which were

goods and purchase supplies.

The daily passenger train, known as the 'Flyer,' came to represent the end of the pioneer era that had begun in New Folden Township so humbly twenty years earlier. As in so many other isolated communities and inland towns, the Soo changed the way of life of the immigrants overnight. Isolation and the struggle to survive far from the life-giving railroad ended, and thriving villages were created. Immigrants of many nationalities arrived, the mail arrived daily, and the world flew by each day as the Flyer made its run for Winnipeg and back. The Soo Line's impact on Newfolden and many other ethnocohesive frontier communities was phenomenal and lasting. Pioneer days were to become just a memory as the graceful 'Flyer' sped daily across the awakening prairie.

Stuart J. Nelson

A freshly-painted Soo Standard 2nd class depot greets the southbound (Eastward) way freight which is in the clear. Soon, it will depart for Thief River Falls. August, 1967

At the turn of the century there were some 60 flour mills along the Soo. Although the railroad brought the world to the frontier, the complex interdependence observed today was many years away. The self sufficiency, often attributed to the frontier, had a lingering death.

214

Leaving Thief River Falls in Pennington County (named after Edmund Pennington, one of the most dynamic of the early Soo presidents), the rails climb a gentle grade to Anita. This is a ghost village that no longer appears on the map but continues to rest upon a glacial moraine. The road then drops as it crosses five beaches of ancient Lake Agassiz to Newfolden where the Middle River is crossed. Middle River is a meandering stream and it almost completely encircles the village of some 345 souls before continuing west to meet the Red River where the waters will flow north to Hudson's Bay. When Lake Agassiz was at its greatest volume, water stood 320 feet deep over Newfolden. The countryside, people and life are well-described in John Tunheim's essay on early settlement in this volume and the entire pioneering environment is meticulously described in his book *A Scandinavian Saga*.

The ancient beaches of Agassiz (called sand ridges by local folk) are the high ground (land) in farming country that today is quite fertile, whereas 100 years ago much of the low country consisted of bogs and marshes requiring drainage to the Middle River.

One can observe from a map that from Detroit Lakes to Lancaster U.S. 59 follows the Soo tracks more or less continually. Crossing the Middle River in our car (or locomotive) we continue northwest through Strandquist (1990 population: 98). Welcome to Karlstad, the first village in Kittson County. This village was named after the Swedish city midway between Oslo and Stockholm. Platted right on the sand of Campbell Beach (of Lake Agassiz), its Scandinavian heritage is as rich as that of Newfolden. From now on the grade will continually drop all the way to Noyes and Winnipeg.

At Lake Bronson the south branch of Two Rivers is crossed. As seen on the plat map, this village was originally platted east of the tracks as Bronson. After the river was dammed east of town the name was changed to reflect the presence of the flood control/recreational lake. Unlike the plat, most of the village has developed west of the tracks. Here one can find the Kittson County Historical Society, a remarkable little jewel of a museum in a town of but 272.

Noyes/Emerson is at the international boundary and on the east bank of the Red River of the North. The elevation here is 792 feet. Noyes was named for J.A. Noyes, a former customs collector and not surprisingly, trains must clear

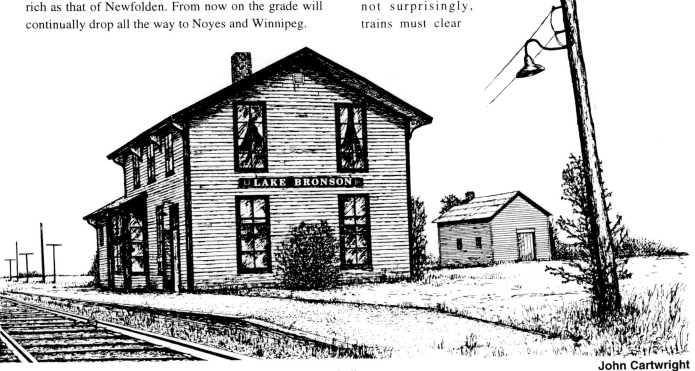

John Cartwright

215

Normally leaving Thief River Falls at 7:30, No. 561 is part of a turn job to the CP interchange at Noyes. Its work done, 6013 is pulling past its caboose and train to get ready to head south as No. 560. July 10, 1992

Charles Bohi

customs here. Until the 1990 CP takeover crews, caboose and locomotives turned back and the Canadian Pacific ran the train on to Winnipeg. Today few trains even have a caboose and the motive power just keeps going–only the Thief River based crew actually turns back . The new Soo (CP) SD 60's are actually made in London Ontario as is most EMD production these days.

Locomotives and entire railroads are truly international in scope and execution. For example: a modern day Soo Line spinoff, the Wisconsin Central Ltd., has purchased the Algoma Central in Ontario out of namesake city Sault Ste. Marie.

Kittson County Historical Society

Above: rebulding the Soo bridge aover the South Branch of Two Rivers at Lake Bronson.

Left: placing girders for one of the original bridge spans at Bronson (Lake Bronson) 1904.

Kittson County Historical Society

Emerson, Manitoba looking south into Minnesota on a late summer evening with a southbound Soo just beyond customs. GN tracks are in the foreground.

Tom Reiersgard Collection

Westside view of joint BN/Soo depot at Noyes . August 11, 1973

Don Mahoney

In the 15 miles between Halma and Lancaster the road drops 90 feet coming down the Campbell beach of ancient Lake Agassiz. From Lancaster to Noyes is 21 miles of down grade 116 feet to the main floor of the Red River Valley.

The small photo shows the main street of Lancaster about 1906 with Soo LIne construction train bunk cars tied up at the siding.

The larger photo shows the windmill, tank, elevators and yards around 1916. Note the gravel ballast.

Lancaster, 1906   **M. W. Hoffman Collection**

Both photos: Kittson County Historical Society

Lancaster, circa 1915.

Above: spiking the rails during the construction of the Winnipeg Line just south of the Canadian border in 1904.

In three generations the Soo was to see the transition from wood burning 4-4-0 locomotives to 2-6-0 Moguls (powered by coal from the eastern states) to ever larger steam power. Engines were purchased new, or built new in the company's own Shoreham shops or were purchased used from other roads as pictured at right.

Wayne Olson Collection

Ex-Rock Island 'Mike' 1031 is all coaled up and ready at Superior's 21st Street roundhouse ca.1949. These engines with their modified Vanderbelt-type tenders saw numerous mine and grain hauling extra assignments in addition to runs to Shoreham and Stevens Point from their Twin Ports home.

Early EMD switching diesels began to appear on the line as early as 1939 and by 1955 the Soo was entirely diesel powered. **2500A & B** pictured here, however, were built as EMD demonstrators in 1949 and delivered to the Soo in May of 1950.

Lake Superior Museum of Transportation

On April 5, 1950 EMD demonstrator EMD **7001** arrived in Duluth on No. 17 from Chicago and turned right back to Minneapolis on No. 63.

This engine covered many Soo Line runs including carrying the Duke and Duchess of Windsor to Portal on No. 4 on April 9. Satisfied with its performance, the Soo purchased this same locomotive in May and numbered it **2500.** The first trip into Duluth as **2500** was on No.17 afterwhich it left on No.18 with the usual five car consist.

On June 8 business car 49 left Minneapolis on No. 8 and set out at Ladysmith. No. 17 with engine **2500** and two extra sleepers picked up 49 with dignitaries that night and arrived in Duluth the morning of June 9 with an 8 car consist.

Standing tall on the left is G.A. Macnamara, Soo Line president 1950-60. 'Mr. Mac' as he was known is shown here with a few directors along with operating, traffic and mechanical department officials.

Conclusion

Three Generations West has attempted to cover new ground in the continuing pictorial history of the western half of the Soo Line Railroad and its antecedent lines. It has been my intention to include fragments of area history over the past one hundred plus years as well as specific histories of essential components to life on, around, in and prior to the railroad's presence.

I have been careful not to duplicate histories which were previously available such as Wallace Abbey's excellent tale of the dieselization of the Soo, 1939-1955, with the additional progress the Soo made into second generation diesel power under the presidency of Leonard Murray. Patrick Dorin's *the Soo Line* remains an excellent overview of Soo operations in the post World War II era and is filled with equipment portraits to aid the modeller.

In the same way it has been my intention that *Three Generations West* be more than merely an addendum to *Saga of the Soo: West from Shoreham.* With the exception of some scattered photographic coverage of snow and wintertime operations the foci of this text have been largely new.

Particularly noteworthy is the pictorial coverage of geology and its interaction with the Soo and humankind. This coverage, much like geology's intrinsic significance to railroads and settlements, is subtle yet widespread. The cut through Minneapolis limestone found on page 14, Patrick Dorin's Cuyuna Range essay and the photo of Hogback Ridge at Balfour are just a few examples. Moreover, attempts have been made to integrate discussions of local geology throughout the text with attention given to individual routes and branches.

For locomotive buffs an effort has been made to place photos of a variety of engines over a long time line without using a roster format. Specifically, engine photo documentation was incidental and should be understood as part of the general story line (*Part I* does have a brief roster section). The evolution of steam engine appendages including the transition of oil burning headlights to electric should now be fairly evident. Additionally, the use of a variety of locomotives on the different lines should now be apparent if one considers the fact that no all-purpose engine like a GP 38-2 existed during the steam era. Similarly, the reader should now understand the regionalization of certain locomotive types for maintenance purposes as a logical and sound practice; e.g. the Baldwin 1500 horsepower road switchers on North Dakota branch lines.

Operations such as coaling, stock trains, icing, ore movements, creameries and the like provide only a glimpse of this line's total operational picture. I hope that the final volume in the *Saga of the Soo* series will be able to provide additional coverage of passenger service, railway mail service, the medical department, maintenance, safety, communications and many other vital components of my favorite portion of my very favorite railroad.

A systematic discussion of depot designs and history is found in *Saga of the Soo Part I* (Frank Vyzralek's article) However; in this volume many photographs of different depots can be found. Additionally, a few John Cartwright line drawings grace the pages along with Russ Porter's delightful painting of the Duluth depot with its slumbering Thief River train. Interior views of depots including the Duluth waiting room and ticket counter are documented, but I surely wish more will show up.

The unfortunate unevenness of photographic quality must be understood in light of the rather extended time frame of camera coverage and the meager population who had cameras and who might have been interested in railroad documentation so many years ago.

July, 1970: John Gjevre

Not the president of the road but nonetheless a most important man: a working conductor completes his reports as the clickity clack of nonwelded rail provides sweet music.

Throughout this volume there has been a purposeful neglect regarding economic strategies, the purchase of the Minneapolis, Northfield and Southern Railway, the acquisition of the Milwaukee Road in 1985 and the take over by the Canadian Pacific in 1990. In the next volume I hope to expand the economic history started in *Saga of the Soo: West from Shoreham* as well as to provide some insight into reasons for the spin offs of such lines as the present day Twin City and Western and the Dakota, Missouri Valley and Western Railways. For those interested in pursuing further research I recommend examining the logic of certain line abandonments. Perhaps a few more years will bring enlightenment as to why the Soo decided to tear up tracks from Pierz to Superior on the old Brooten Line. Today the only Twin Cities to Duluth train service is over the Burlington Northern's former GN line. Precarious at best, this situation provides a bottleneck and a potential national disaster. Additional studies of Soo advertising methods and a comprehensive history of lines in Wisconsin and Upper Michigan are also needed. Let us hope that such stories will be forthcoming from the members of the Soo Line Historical and Technical Society.

While the dependence of the settler and his or her interdependency with the railroad is stressed in Father Bill Sherman's chapter, frontier life prior to the Soo and the evolution of the immigrant settlement and society as the railroad was to come is covered in John Tunheim's essay. Additionally, Mrs. Monroe's family history of depot life, although a personal history, contributes greatly to our general understanding of life along the rails. We are most thankful to the kindness of these very busy yet well-versed individuals to share their special expertise and interests with us.

Change indeed is a constant and the CP/Soo changes and will change as it continues to roll on. For many these changes are difficult and painful. One must acknowledge and confront this uncertainty with a ampule of sadness. Nonetheless the Soo has been and will remain part of the varied fabric of the Upper Midwest. It is a line that crosses, connects and serves the steppes and prairies of North Dakota, the lakes, parklands and farm country of Minnesota as well as the forests and woods, rivers, dairies and industries of Wisconsin. It serves an increasingly international crowd, comprised not only of Canada and the United States, but of the whole world. Through the Port of Duluth as well as coast to coast on container trains from the Orient, Europe and elsewhere, the CP/Soo plays a pivotal role in today's global economy. Although not stated in the text, it is interesting to note that the Soo Line owned Great Lakes Steamship lines which were operated from 1892 to 1915 through various subsidiaries. Some ex-Soo ships served with the Merchant Marine during World War II and at least one was eventually sold to a French shipping company. (See "Memories for Love of a Railroad"; *Soo Liner* 2nd & 3rd quarters 1983). The future of the CP/Soo depends on continued interaction with a complex international marketplace.

Acknowledgements

It is unlikely that this volume would have ever been written had it not been for the steadfast love and encouragement of my wife Marjorie. Moreover, the scope and depth of photographic coverage in this volume would have been limited greatly without her eagerness to travel with me in the quest for Soo photos, knowledge and historical tidbits. During 1994 alone she accompanied me on 11 research trips to many points in North and South Dakota, Minnesota and Wisconsin covering a total of 7242 miles.

Stuart Nelson's encyclopedic knowledge of Soo history and wealth of material is matched only by his generous reciprocity of them to myself and others interested in the Soo. Similarly, the late Wayne Olsen of Duluth had files upon files of photos and prime source information that have contributed immensely to the coverage of northeastern Minnesota and the Duluth Superior area.

John Bergene of the Soo Line (CP-Heavy Haul U.S.) Corporate Communications department has been munificent with his time and encouragement of this ongoing project which covers Soo Line history, Minnesota and westward.

To my contributing authors, John Tunheim, Father Bill Sherman, Carol Monroe and Pat Dorin go my especial thanks for taking time from their very busy lives to conceive chapters from their individual areas of expertise for our enjoyment.

Dr. Al Ohrt not only provided some excellent postcard coverage of vintage Soo history, but also provided leads to the whereabouts of Gene Foote, Paul Carlson, Gordon Twedt, Daryl Thompson and many others who had good photos from the 1920s and earlier.

In addition to the postcard views of Gordon Twedt, we also enjoy views from the collections of Pete Bonesteel, Ron Olin, Ed Wertheim, Douglas Wick and others. Incidentally, Douglas Wick's definitive history of placenames in North Dakota was used as a major secondary source for much of the detail data on North Dakota towns which appear in this volume.

Larry Fisher's talents can be appreciated in the cover art, the frontpiece and the beautiful painting of a station stop with a one-car local on page 77. Gratitude must also be expressed to Russ Porter and John Cartwright for allowing their wonderful depot paintings and drawings to be included. All of these contributions help to remind us that good art can ressurect a special dimension of history otherwise unobtainable.

Lawrence Drabus and other Soo Line veterans have increased my understanding of operations and provided some unique historic photos. The following museums and historical societies were helpful in a variety of ways - including providing prime source material as well as photographic and graphic coverage.

Minnesota Historical Society
State Historical Society of North Dakota
State Historical Society of Wisconsin
Institute for Regional Studies (at NDSU)
Becker County Historical Society.
Crosby (ND) Museum
Douglas County Museum
Grant County Hisorical Society
Hankinson Depot Museum (James Fischer)
Kittson County Museum
Lake Superior Museum of Transport
Pope County Museum
Soo Line Historical and Technical Society

* * *

Color photos from Richard Yaremko, Otto Dobnick, Lloyd Berger, Andy Sutherland, J. David Ingles, Bob Kjelland, Cory Tryan, Byron Knutson, Richard Logan, Bill Flint, the Soo Line/CP Railroad and others are also appreciated.

Bill Flint requires special recognition for redrawing and labeling all the grade elevation drawings found on the bottom of nine pages as well as the maps of the Enderlin and Thief River Falls yards at the close of the steam era.

Mary Sjue deserves gratitude for her efforts in providing much of the Portal material. Don Mahoney's efforts in contributing several photographs, including an outstanding 1916 threshing rig shot at Spiral, ND have also been appreciated in addition to his retelling of his adventure as a student telegrapher.

Permission to reprint the essay letter by Richard Hofstrand, Ph.D on cattle shipments in 1912 has given *Three Generations West* a unique flavor that the reader should also appreciate in his whole volume; *With Affection Marten.*

To Helen Stoner we acknowledge her gracious permission to use copyrighted material from the Outlook/Daleview Diamond Jubilee book.

I'm certain I have missed dozens of others who were helpful and generous with source material; we all benefit by the sharing of many to provide the special insight I hope this book will contribute into life along and within in the Soo for the past one hundred and more years.

Almost last, but certainly not least, an enormous thanks to my son Peter who did the typesetting and page layout design on a Macintosh computer. He thoughtfully edited the entire volume and has given continual stylistic input throughout the course of writing. Final laser output was produced by Dianne Haugen (Whiskey Creek Documents) whose experience and insights have been beneficial to both Peter and myself. Finally, Sandra Carlson's efforts in the individual artwork and paging are also appreciated.

Bibliography ————

Books:

Abbey, Wallace W., *The Little Jewel* . Pueblo, CO: Pinon Publications, 1984.

Bluemle, John, *The Face of North Dakota, Rev. Ed.* Bismarck: North Dakota Geological Survey, 1991.

Dorin, Patrick, *The Soo Line.* Seattle: Superior Publishing, 1979.

Goodey, Brian & Eidem, R.J. *Readings in the Geography of North Dakota.* Bismarck: North Dakota Studies, 1968.

Hudson, John C. *Plains Country Towns.* Minneapolis: University of Minnesota Press, 1985

Hyde, Frederick W., *Soo Line 1993 Review.* Denver, CO: HyRail Productions, 1993

Minneapolis, St. Pauls amd Sault Ste Marie Ry Official Industrial Guide 1905-06 Minneapolis.

Prosser, Richard, *Rails to the North Star.* Minneapolis: Dillon Press, 1966.

Suprey, Leslie, *Steam Trains of the Soo.* Fortuna, CA: Humboldt, 1984.

Tunheim, John R., *A Scandinavian Saga.* Privately printed, 1984.

Upham, Warren, *Minnesota Geographic Place Names.* Minnesota Historical Society (reprinted), 1969.

Wick, Douglas, *North Dakota Place Names.* Bismarck: Hedemarken Collectibles, 1988.

Willard, Daniel E. *The Story of the North Star State.* St. Paul: Webb Publishing, 1922.

Willard, Daniel E. *The Story of the Prairies. (9th edition).* Kalamazoo, MI: Ihling Bros./Everard Co., 1921

Wishek, Nina Farley, *Along the Trails of Yesterday.* Ashley (ND): Tribune, 1941.

Other books listed in the bibliography of *Part I* may also be helpful.

Annuals:

Annual reports of the M. St. P. & S. S. M. Ry; the M. St. P & S. S. M. RR; the Soo Line Railroad Company; and the Canadian Pacific Railway - various years.
Moody's Transportation Manual and Poor's Manual.

Documents:

Minnesota Historical Society, St. Paul is a repository for many obsolete records of the company through the years and was utilized for much of the prime source material. In addition, most of the newspapers in the state of Minnesota are available on microfilm through the Historical Society and I was able to view some of these at the Moorhead Public Library through interlibrary loan.

Soo Line Historical and Technical Society has extensive files which I found very helpful. For the new generation of scholars they are in the process of cataloging and filing copies and originals of all company 'Authorization For Expenditures' and these will be housed in the University of Wisconsin–Oshkosh library. The State Historical Society of North Dakota and the Institute for Regional Studies in Fargo also have considerable primary source material.

Articles and Magazines:

Soo Liner Magazine published by the M. St. P. & S. S. M. RR from 1950 to 1960 and by the Soo Line Railroad from 1961 to 1989. *The SOO* published quarterly since 1977 by the Soo Line Historical and Technical Society.

Multiple articles have been published by *TRAINS Magazine, RAILROAD magazine* and *RAILFAN and RAILROAD magazine* through the years. *Diesel Era* published a two part series on Soo Line diesels in 1995. *Passenger Train Journal* also did a series on Soo Line varnish (not covered in this volume, but in *Part I* and will also be found in the forthcoming third volume).

Vyzralek, Frank, et.al. *North Dakota's Depots, Standardization on the Soo Line,* N.D. History Vol. 42 #4 1975 p9 ff.

INDEX VOLUME II

Back page: Eastbound ethylene glycol train under the BN Hi Line bridge near Valley City.

Robert Kjelland